MAXIMISING

**No problem can be
conscious**

– Albert Einstein, Physicist & Nobel Laureate (1879 - 1955)

T.O.A.S.T.

A Conscious Thinking Approach

How to Recognise, Maximise and Celebrate
What You Have to Get What You Want

MUYIWA OLUMOROTI

T.O.A.S.T.

A Conscious Thinking Approach

A personal development resource
developed for
PROFSEXPERTS
by
MUYIWA OLUMOROTI

WORD2PRINT

TOAST – A Conscious Thinking Approach

First published in the United Kingdom in 2016 by
Word2Print
www.word2print.com
ISBN: 978-1-908588-08-1

A CIP catalogue record for this title is available from the
British Library

Typesetting by Michael Babatunde @ Supreme Core
Media, UK

Printed by
CPI Group UK (Croydon),
England. UK

Contents

Permissions

The author gratefully acknowledges the following individuals and organisations for granting permission to use their material and images in sections of this book:

Albert Einstein (en.wikipedia.org)

Aare Afe Babalola

Ayodeji Ayeola images X7 (Ayodeji Ayeola)

Ben Carson (bigstockphoto.com)

Bennett Olson (Mr Bennett Olson)

Bill Gates (commons.wikimedia.org)

Chief Obafemi Awolowo (S.A.N.) (1909–1987)

David Beckham OBE (bigstockphoto.com)

Demis Hassabis (www.wired.co.uk)

Do Won Chang (brainprick.com)

Li Ka-Shing (en.wikipedia.org)

Mark Zukerberg (bigstockphoto.com)

Martin Luther King Jr. (en.wikipedia.org)

Mary Kay Ash (commons.wikimedia.org)

Mother Teresa (commons.wikimedia.org)

Nelson Mandela (www.flickr.com)

Nick D'Aloisio (www.wsj.com)

Oprah Gail Winfrey (bigstockphoto.com)

Shahid Khan (commons.wikimedia.org)

Steve Jobs (bigstockphoto.com)

Vicky Pryce (commons.wikimedia.org)

Dedication

I dedicate this book to boys and girls, men and women who know that they have much to give to their world and are striving hard to achieve the purpose for which they were created.

Foreword

I am privileged and honoured to write the foreword to this book. I first met Dr Muyiwa Olumoroti in London at a birthday party held in my honour in 2015. He is a colleague of my cousin, Dr Patricia Olowu, who had told me a lot of complimentary things about him before the party.

As a lawyer, I am constantly on the lookout for any comprehensive guide on how to maximise my potentials in this increasingly fast-paced and competitive world. Knowing that Dr Olumoroti is a psychiatrist who is also involved in coaching, mentoring and teaching on leadership, empowerment and emotional intelligence, I was particularly interested in the insights he may have on the subject. Having read '*T.O.A.S.T. - A Conscious Thinking Approach*', I must confess that I have found in this book a framework for anyone who wants to prepare for the future and stand out from the crowd.

Long ago, Benjamin Disraeli (21 December 1804–19 April 1881) who twice served as Prime Minister of the Britain said, "One secret of success in life is for a man to be ready for his opportunity when it comes." These words are just as appropriate today as they were in Disraeli's time. In my view, to be "ready" entails being aware of the "Talents", the "Abilities", "Skills" and "Time", and employing them profitably. When these aforementioned factors converge with "Opportunity", the inevitable result will be the examples of success referred to in this book.

In our fast-paced modern world, we are often left

time-crunched, overwhelmed and stressed as we sprint towards the finish line. We are often too busy to realise our talents, the opportunities that present themselves, our abilities and skills. Many people fail to realise that time is an irreplaceable resource and often fritter it away. Dr Olumoroti seeks to re-orientate our thought processes in order to guide us toward achieving our true potentials.

I assure you that you are about to read a unique and life changing book.

Mr Adedapo Tunde-Olowu, LL.M, FCIArb, FCTI
Legal Practitioner
(Admitted in Nigeria and England and Wales)
Partner (Dispute Resolution Group,
AELEX, Lagos, Nigeria)

Introduction

I was in the middle of writing the manuscript of my book *'40 Secrets to Relevance: How to Avoid being Overlooked, Bypassed or Ignored'* when I received an invitation to speak on 'Standing Out From the Crowd' at a youth programme in Poole, south England. On the one hand, I thought that this would be a great opportunity to impart the knowledge I had to the young people, some of whom I had met previously at another conference. On the other hand, I thought by accepting that invitation, I had put myself into a situation in which I would have to work very hard in order for me to really 'stand out', given the theme of that event. Also, being scheduled to be the last speaker on the day, after lunch, would certainly make my task more difficult. I knew that from experience.

A lot of questions ran through my mind: Should I look for yellow trousers, a purple jacket, a pair of white shoes and red socks to wear on that day in order to really stand out? Or should I head for a perfume shop and purchase a fragrance with a very strong but beautiful scent so that the participants could fix their noses on me throughout my presentation and talk? Or better still, should I wear a red hat with rings on small bells around the rim so that I could really get noticed with all the noise that would follow my every movement as I deliver my speech? The organisation that invited me was definitely not looking for a clown, and I knew I had to come up with something tangible very quickly.

Fortunately, I had developed an approach for dealing

with situations such as this – and that is, to first look inwards for what I already had that could be used to solve a problem, move me forward, or get me out of a tight situation. The other manuscript that I was working on at the time was 'TOAST – A Conscious Thinking Approach'. I thought that with this, I would really stand out from the crowd. Taking TOAST with me to a youth meeting would either get me noticed or make me a laughing stock. One of these was guaranteed!

This book, *TOAST – A Conscious Thinking Approach*, is the summary of my thoughts, experiences, research and the speeches which I delivered at that youth meeting. Most of the participants were shocked to hear some of the information I gave them during the sessions. Many were annoyed with themselves that they have hidden treasures in their lives and were not doing something about any of them. At the end, we (and that includes me) all left the meeting, refreshed, re-energised and refocused to make the best out of life.

We all have weaknesses, and there are various external factors and threats that want to mitigate our ability to maximise our potential. But rather than be preoccupied with those limiting factors or what we don't have, we need to focus on what we have in order to move forward. There are at least five things, among others, that most people have, and if care is not taken, will go to waste without them knowing it. I have encapsulated these inside T.O.A.S.T. - Talents (and gifts), Opportunities, Abilities (and strengths), Skills and Time.

Everybody has TOAST; you just have to think about them. What you already have is all you will need to get what you don't have and that includes everything you will ever require to negotiate life. I sincerely wish that you will find the content of this resource useful and also be in a position to pass it on to benefit others.

Muyiwa Olumoroti
London, England

Acknowledgements

The acronym T.O.A.S.T. and the material in this book have been inspired and sustained by God over a period of time. I am forever grateful to Him for seeing me through to the completion of the work. My sincere gratitude also goes to my wife Kemi and children Wonu, Tomisin and Anjola for their support and patience when I had to constantly keep them interested in the TOAST concept.

I also want to thank many of my associates, colleagues and friends who have taken out time to look at the manuscript and offer valuable suggestions to improve the content of the book. I hereby express my sincere appreciation to Dr Patricia Olowu, Dr Kayode Osanaiye, Dr Onikepe Ijete, Pastor Edirin Atumah, Seyi Oyediran, Karis Kolawole, Ferdinard Lawson, Mrs Kemi Oyedepo, Florence Nakkozi, Stella Kizito, Egness Masango, and to Professor Temitayo Shokunbi of the College of Medicine, University of Ibadan for taking time out of their very busy schedules to comment on the manuscript. I am eternally grateful to Mr Adedapo Tunde-Olowu, who though I had only known for a short period of time, agreed and wrote a most befitting foreword for TOAST.

I thank Kemi Oyesola for the wonderful editorial work and Michael Babatunde of Supreme Core Media for the typesetting. Adeola Disu of Established Designs did an excellent job on the book cover. I am greatly indebted to individuals and organisations who have given permissions for their work to be cited or used in one form or the other. I thank you all.

*"What you already have
is all you will need
to get what you don't have;
and, that includes everything
you will ever require
to negotiate life."*

-Muyiwa Olumoroti

You Are Hired! The story of Bennett Olson

Bennett Olson was an unemployed 22 year-old man who paid 300 US Dollars to put his face and name on a billboard in Minneapolis, Minnesota with the plea 'Hire Me!' Prospective employers were impressed by his initiative and entrepreneurial spirit. Shortly afterwards, the vice president of GKS Services spoke to him on the phone and later scheduled an interview for him. The billboard led to some attention and other interviews. Olson later took a job at Laser Design & GKS Services, a 3D scanning company in Bloomington. This is what Olson said in his own words: "I kind of like doing different things not being the regular guy who does the same old stuff." Bennett Olson could have used the money he had to gamble, buy drugs or drink alcohol to drown the sorrow of unemployment. But he chose to use what he had to get what he wanted. Mr Olson later worked as a Field Engineer at MSpace, Greater Minneapolis-St. Paul Area, US. Wise man indeed! http://www.bennett-olson.com

PART 1

THE MOST IMPORTANT QUESTIONS

Chapter 1

Why 'Thinking' and Why 'Conscious'?

Why Thinking?

One of the most important functions of the human mind is to think. As a man thinks, so will his life turn out to be. A man's life will always go in the direction of his thoughts. According to research, the average number of thoughts that go through the human mind each hour is about 2,500. Imagine 2,500 students of a large comprehensive college *entering* and *running* through your mind in just one hour. Some researchers have cited figures in the range of 50-70,000 thoughts per day for the average person. That is a huge number of thought-work for the human mind over a 24-hour period.

If you were able to sell each of your thoughts, even for a penny a thought, you would be rich in no time. However many of these thoughts are useless and unimportant thoughts, and they pass through the mind at fast speeds, giving little or no time to really 'think' about them – like when you are bathing, picking up a cloth from the floor or entering your car.

However, a significant number of the thoughts that pass through our minds are specific, measurable and directed, and they can be channelled towards purposeful activities. However, these thoughts are not automatic; you have to think them through, you have to capture them, and you have to process them for tangible use. You do have control over what you think about and only you can truly think these thoughts in order to solve a problem, move forward or attain greater heights in life.

I must also add quickly that you have a choice whether your thoughts are good or bad, pleasant or horrible. You can control your thoughts, and you cannot leave your thoughts for others to think for you. If you leave the task of your thinking to other people, you will surely lose control over your life and will never maximise your potential.

Why 'Conscious'?

No problem can be solved from the same level of consciousness that created it.

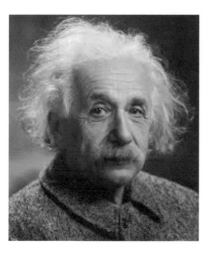

This statement was credited to the great physicist and Nobel Laureate, Albert Einstein (1879 –1955). In other words, we cannot solve problems by using the same kind of thinking or awareness that we used when the problem was first created. So, to solve a problem, you have to use your mind to think differently, deeper, higher, and 'more thoughtfully', in order to perform better, to improve and to attain new heights.

How can we solve a problem? What strategies are there to solve a problem? The first thing to do is to ask the right questions by first defining what the problem is. So ask, "What's the problem? Why is it a problem? What effect is the problem having? What desired effect do I want? How will I get there (the solution)? What do I need to solve the problem? What do I do first, and what is next in the process?" And then next, and next. Problems don't just disappear; it takes thoughtful processes to arrive at solutions and desirable outcomes.

The core message of TOAST – *A Conscious Thinking Approach* is this: if you want to prepare for the future, if you want to stand out from the crowd and be relevant, if you don't want life to pass you by, you have to look inside you (some people call this introspective thinking), and give the best of what you have. Don't look for what you don't have; use what you have already: prepare it, improve it, package it and deploy it. The latter four actions all involve conscious elements in their execution.

"If you want to prepare for the future, if you want to stand out from the crowd and be relevant you have to look inside you."
-Muyiwa Olumoroti

Unfortunately, a lot of people are looking for that 'extra something' in order to be the extraordinary person they should be while they neglect and fail to nurture what they have already. But to really stand out and be counted, you have to consider and consciously think about what you have already. Needless to say, you need to be conscious of these things if anything great is to happen for you.

Conscious thinking doesn't come to you naturally. The journey of consciousness demands that you are deliberate about it, focus on it, and let the ideas flow from inside you. You are more aware when you are conscious in your thinking and when you make every effort to remain aware of what you are thinking about. You are conscious when you deliberately question your thoughts, when you challenge your ideas, when you think outside the box, and when you change the rules of the game in your favour.

How will I know when I am conscious? Very simple: when you are conscious, you are actively thinking. Events don't just happen for no reason; there is a connection to everything, there is a goal in mind, there is a process, and there is an expected outcome or a destination. You just don't do nothing or anything and land just anywhere or arrive at some place in the middle of nowhere. You have a target, you focus, and you are deliberate. That way, you are conscious.

You can control what you consciously think about with your mind. One of the best ways to think consciously is to write down your thoughts, imaginations and ideas. Don't allow them to just fly around your head. You must capture your thoughts, and what came out of your thinking. Write them down somewhere, and think about them. Think about them again, and turn your thoughts into workable ideas. This will give you clarity, refine your ideas and make you progress further.

You have to find time for conscious thinking and conscious living. So it is important to consciously think about what you think about. Your mind is only fully working when you consciously engage it. Don't stop at thinking; do something today. Even a small shift might prove to be a significant move. As you do this, many things will change in your life for the better. Even you will be amazed about what you can achieve.

Chapter 2

Why T.O.A.S.T?

Why T.O.A.S.T?

The New versus the Old

I have heard people say something like this: "Life's too complicated these days; I'd rather go back to the old times!" And really, you can't blame them. Life in the old times was more predictable; society valued respect, human dignity and life than we do today. Also, there was less threat of uncertainties, terrorism, global warming, mass unemployment and other societal ills that we see today; at least not as much as today. But what do we have today? A lot of arm struggle, people living longer with less resources to support them, the Age of the Machine – with loss of jobs; and fast and modern technology that is becoming too fast for man. But only you can answer this question, whatever your perspective: 'Would you rather live in the New World or the Old World?'

Many people alive today are in a peculiar situation–having experienced the Old World and now living in the New World; or as Wayne Malcolm* puts it - the "Old Game and the New

---

*Bishop Wayne Malcolm, a leading performance coach is the founder and president of the International Coaching Achievers Network (ICAN).

Game." This is what the Old World is like: You are born, and you grow from one box to another – from womb box to a cot box (hospital), to house box or nursery, to classroom or school box - from primary school to secondary school to college and to university (if you decide to go there). And once you leave the school box, you are expected to go into an office box (or some other work environment). If you are fortunate (or rather unfortunate) enough, you may be given a moving box (a bicycle or company car), and after a few pay cheques, you are expected to get married or boxed in with a total stranger (absolutely nothing wrong with that – stranger box) to live together forever or for as long as you can. Then when you die (all of us will, at some point), you are put in a wooden, metal or plastic box, and sent to the great beyond! What a life!

In the New World, once you are born, you decide to stay outside the boxes of life as much as you can. You discover the talents you have been endowed with, and decide to do something with your talents and gifts, the opportunities that you have, your abilities and strengths. In other words, you use your time wisely and deliver what is on the inside of you with your skills. You must however know boxes for what they really are – they want to limit you! But you must not allow them to hedge you in, because life continues, whether you do or you don't.

For too long, people have been miseducated. Many have been told to go to school, get a certificate or earn a degree, look for a job, and then be tied down to a lifestyle of jobs (sometimes toil and misery), running from pay cheque to pay cheque, and competing in a rat-race which nobody eventually wins. Life generally wants to put you in a box. You have a responsibility to resist it. The Old World wants to make you follow a set pattern in order to service the system, the oligarchs, and the multinationals. You have a responsibility to free yourself from it.

People living in the New World know very well that life (as we know it) will never go back to the Old World again – and they decide to look inwards rather than outwards. They refuse to wait for their parents, their spouse, their school, their boss or their government to determine or dictate how they live their lives. They make a decision to use what God has endowed them with, to make head way in life.

According to the *Invading The Seven Mountains* document (Tommi Femrite, 2008) from the Wagner Leadership Institute (http://www.wagnerleadership. org), to live successfully in the New World, you have to climb one or more of the seven mountains of influence: Religion, Family, Education, Government, Media, Arts, and Entertainment and Business – and you need your Talents and gifts, Opportunities, Abilities and strengths, Skills and Time at your disposal at every corner and stage.

"Nothing will change in your life until you actually do something about it."

It is not enough to just know about TOAST. A conscious thinking approach to TOAST is crucial to maximising your potential. You have to capture this on paper, on tablets, and on your computers, and hold on to them. TOAST will work for you in any situation and in all fields of endeavour. You must be conscious of what you have and keep them in view all the time. You must go beyond thinking and put the components of T-O-A-S-T into practice on a daily basis. Your success and ascension to higher heights will depend on the daily changes that you make. Think and meditate on these things.

Chapter 3

Why 'Me' or Why 'You'?

Do Won Chang is the founder of the clothing retail store Forever 21. When Do Won Chang moved to America, he worked as a janitor, in coffee shops and pumping gas stations. Credited with the power of observation, while working in a petrol station, Chang noticed that the most expensive cars were driven by fashion retailers. He and his wife later opened a clothing store blocks away from the one-bedroom flat where their family lived. Today he is worth around $5 billion.

Mother Teresa was born as Anjezë Gonxhe Bojaxhiu on 26 August 1910 at Skopje, now capital of the Republic of Macedonia. Her father died in 1919 when she was only eight years old. Her mother later raised her as a Roman Catholic. Mother Teresa made a decision early in life, to commit herself to a religious life and left home at age 18 to join the Sisters of Loreto as a missionary. Although mostly known, (and sometimes criticised) for her humanitarian and missionary work, Mother Teresa worked as a teacher and then as a headmistress. Moved by the

poverty surrounding her in Calcutta, India, she received what she described as a 'call' (or an order) to leave her convent to help the poor by living among them. Her mission took her to work with the low of the lows of society, the terminally ill, the destitute and the starving. She was later awarded the Nobel Peace Prize in 1979. Although starting with nothing, Mother Teresa became an international icon of her generation through the gift of kindness she was endowed with.

David Beckham OBE. The retired English footballer, is a household name that many people will recognise around the world. But his ascension to fame and popularity, if not careful, will almost mask the humble background that Beckham came from. Born to fanatical Manchester United FC supporters Sandra Georgina (hair dresser) and David Edward Alan Beckham (kitchen fitter), Beckham attended footballing schools and won a competition to take part in a training session at FC Barcelona before signing on as a trainee at Manchester United on July 8 1991.

Many who are accustomed with David Beckham's achievements may not have noticed the ups and downs that characterised his early career; he was at one point loaned to Preston North End, a Third Division side during part of the 1994–95 season to get some first team experience. On his return to Manchester United, Beckham quickly established himself as a major force, and helped his team to win major titles.

Mary Kay Ash (born May 12, 1918) was a woman who turned disappointments around to fulfill her destiny. A product of a fairly privileged upbringing, her mother was a nurse and later, a restaurant manager. Ash married at the age of 17 shortly after graduating from high school in 1934. Her first marriage lasted for only 10 years. She then went to work for Stanley Home Products but left after she was passed for promotion in favour of a man she had trained. She intended to write a book to help women in business but this turned into a business plan. Sadly, one month before Ash and her new husband George Arthur Hallenbeck were to start Beauty (later Mary Kay Cosmetics), Hallenbeck died of a heart attack. Despite the setbacks, Mary Kay Ash pursued her dreams, and in the process, set millions of women (and men) on a life of sufficiency and financial independence. Her secrets were her reliance on God, and her marketing and people skills.

You may already be asking the questions 'Why me?' and 'Why all these names – Do Won Chang, Mother Teresa, David Beckham and Mary Kay Ash?' 'Why me and what have these people got to do with me, or TOAST?' It might actually help you if I first address this question to myself and state it very clearly that: "No one is responsible for my life except me." The same thing applies to you. 'Why you' is because only 'You' can change the course of your life. No matter what has happened to you in the past or what will happen to you in the future, there is so much people can do for you or offer to help you with. In the end you will have to channel the course of your own life.

There is something therapeutic and comforting in assuming that if one is born with a silver spoon into an affluent family or a stable democracy, life would be a bed of roses. This is not a certainty. It is equally 'soothing' to have a bad situation to blame for our various predicaments. But life, in my experience, doesn't understand or tolerate excuses. You may have been the product of a teenage pregnancy or grown up in a single parent family, have a disability (or handicap) or one disadvantage or the other, or in fact be born in the Third World, in a remote corner in one of the most deprived parts of the world. These seemingly negative attributes will definitely try to limit you from progressing but the only thing that can limit you is 'You'.

The other examples below will drive home some of the points that I am trying to pass across. As you read, I want you to note and write down what you think is common to all these people.

Oprah Gail Winfrey is well known for her popular Oprah Winfrey Show. Oprah was born into poverty in rural Mississippi to a teenage single mother. She faced childhood adversity and became pregnant at the age of 14 but lost the child in infancy. Starting from a job in radio and later anchoring the local evening news, she grew, via her talk show to become a host, a producer, an actress, and a media mogul. Today her net worth is close to $3 billion, and as of the time of writing, she was North America's only black billionaire. All she did was to use the gifts, talents and abilities she has been endowed with by God.

Shahid Khan is the Pakistani-born American billionaire who owns the Jacksonville Jaguars of the National Football League (NFL) and the English Premier League team Fulham F.C. When he first arrived in the United States from Pakistan, he reportedly spent his first night in the US in a $2 a night room at the University

YMCA hostel. His first job was reported as washing dishes for $1.20 an hour. After an engineering degree from the University of Illinois, he designed a revolutionary one-piece truck bumper and later went into auto part manufacturing. Today he is worth over $4 billion. Mr Khan is a man who knew how to maximise the opportunities that came his way, despite all the obstacles he had to overcome.

Li Ka-shing was forced to leave school before the age of 15 after his father's death. He found a job in a plastics trading company where he laboured 16 hours a day. He later started his own company in 1950, manufacturing plastics, and then went into real estate investment. His net worth in November 2015 is reported to be $34 billion. What component(s) of TOAST helped Ka-shing to maximise his potential?

The late **Steve Jobs** was abandoned by his parents when he was young and was adopted as an infant later by Clara and Paul Jobs. Jobs had frustration with formal school education as a child and following high school dropped out of college after six months. He later went on to pursue his passion for computers and became one of the greatest innovators of the modern world. Next time you hold an iPod, an iPhone or an iPad, think of Steve Jobs. His innovative skills made him a *primus inter pares* (first among equals) in his field of endeavour.

Something in common

Before you read further, check what you have written down as being common to these people. You may have three, four or more:

Common factor 1:

Common factor 2:

Common factor 3:

Common factor 4:

A quick examination of the different examples given above reveals something common to most of them; and that is the ability to identify what they like and enjoy doing, and persistence with it to the point of near-perfection. For example, David Beckham was a workaholic who spent thousands of hours practising his trademark free kicks.

Bill Gates, another example, spent thousands of hours writing software codes. The Beatles performed for months on end in Berlin, playing marathon gigs well before they became world famous. These people all worked long hours on something they enjoyed, long before realising this 'something' would lead to success. It is not enough to just identify what you are good at, mastery of the talent or trade is equally important in addition to virtue of persistence.

What about you and me?

I could go on and on, but that may not serve you any useful purpose if I don't explain how this applies to you, and to me. So, again, why you? It is because your story may not be different from any of the people listed above. In fact, you may fare better than them at the beginning. These people faced their respective challenges in life but only used whatever they had to achieve great feats in order to be where they are today. Some did not set out to become wealthy or famous but they continued to work on what they enjoyed, improving along the process, and moving to the next stage and found success. Some of their success stories can be likened to digging a well and then reaching water. Considerable effort, determination and persistence are necessary at the beginning and along the way.

It can be relieving or even very comforting if we can all find someone else, a situation or an event to blame for the position in life in which we find ourselves but these arguments or excuses can only be sustained for a short while. You will soon find out, sometimes harshly, that you are solely responsible for the outcomes of your life. This hard truth might in fact make you think again.

We are all victims of circumstances, but how then do we turn our circumstances into something more pleasurable, fulfilling, rewarding, and satisfying? However you want to consider or interprete your circumstance – good, fair, comfortable, poor, bad - the quest for change in humans cannot be quenched. This quest leads to wishes, hunger, thirst and sometimes, desperation. We all desire to get better. Whether from point A to B, A to G, F to M, or S to Z- one thing is constant - a desire or wish, for most people, to get better and not remain in the same position for too long.

Whilst some have given up and accepted the status quo, some are working to change their conditions while others are not sure whether they can achieve breakthrough. The good news is that TOAST will provide a framework with which you can start to provide solutions to circumstances that you are in and the challenges that you face every day. By embracing TOAST today, you are maximising the potential you have to achieve a great future.

Your beginning or present circumstance is irrelevant only if you can maximise your TOAST in aiming at the future. When it comes to the future, you must know where you are going, how you are going to get there and what it takes to get there. The Talents, the Opportunities, the Abilities, the Time and the Skills available to you and possessed by every individual are what TOAST is all about. The components of TOAST are parts of what you should think about in order to maximise your potential. Think about it today and surprise yourself. Just do it!

PART 2:

TOAST- A CONSCIOUS THINKING APPROACH

Chapter 4

T
Talents

Talents

Definition: Something given; a present. Talent by definition is innate ability.

T alents by their very nature are given and endowed. Gifts have nothing to do with your qualification or performance or experience. You are born with talents and gifts (they are innate), and you did not do anything to possess or deserve them. Let me first make it clear from the onset here what many people struggle to consider or accept, and that is: you have a gift (or gifts) and are endowed with talents. God has never created a man or woman without equipping them with what they need to negotiate life or what they require to excel. God has provided you with everything that you need to fulfil the purpose of your life. You just have to discover them.

Among the many attributes that could give a man or woman substance, worth or acclaim, and make them shine in life are the gifts and the talents they possess. Gifts and talents are expressed in the way a person thinks, feels, behaves, and acts. It makes them achieve certain feats not easily attained by those not endowed with such gifts. Talents that are intangible (not physically seen, touched or sensed in other ways) are often ignored or underestimated. Many people limit gifts and talents to attributes that are obvious to onlookers or things that produce performance; and when they cannot do certain things as well as others, they conclude that they don't have gifts or talents. Nothing can be further from the truth.

Amazingly, when I ask some people what gifts or talents they possess, they often pause, keep quiet for a moment, look into space, or scratch their head and say things like: "I don't know", "It's hard to say" or "I think I can do this or that." My experience is that the moment I start to point out various examples of gifts and talents to people, they then start to say "I have this", "I'm very good at that", or "I didn't realise that this is a gift", or "I didn't know that was what you were referring to." It is obvious most of time that these people have never sat down at any point to ask themselves some very important questions: "What is my gift? What talent(s) do I have?" Or, "how do I use them?" Sometimes, people need help to identify these talents, which is what this book is about.

Ridiculously simple

I read about the story of a factory that manufactures soap. It happened that some of the soap boxes at the end of the production line were empty. Staff found out that the problem was from the assembly line, and the company called in engineers to fix it. The company spent time and money to install high resolution X-ray monitors* to watch the boxes to make sure they were not empty. But a factory worker came up with a simple idea – he installed a powerful industrial fan to blow off the assembly line any empty box not containing soap. The empty boxes were then collected at the end of the day and recycled. How did the foreman come up with that idea? Well, some people just have a talent for coming up with brilliant ideas and solutions.

*X-ray monitors can detect empty soap boxes on the assembly line but another device has to remove them.

Question: What do you think would have happened if the X-ray monitors picked up empty boxes on the assembly line?

Answer: Another device would have to be installed to knock the empty boxes off the line to be collected later, just as is the case with the industrial fan. But industrial fans are far cheaper than high resolution X-ray monitors.

An everyday thing

Talents and gifts are not that difficult to understand; we use them every day. Unless you are conscious of these gifts, you will not maximise your potential. The gifts that I am referring to include:

- Spiritual gifts to know and solve complex problems.

- Gifts of insight. Some of these are included in spiritual gifts. They include gifts of knowledge (exceptional ability to know), of understanding (including of very deep and complex things), of solving enigmas and of resolving conundrums.

- Gift of wisdom (in how to apply knowledge) and of compassion.

- Performing gifts and talents, such as musical abilities, singing, acting, poetry, comedy, chess, sports and operation in numbers.

- Creative gifts such as in arts, crafts, design,

arrangements, imagery, drawing, and architecture.

- Gift for exceptional imagination and reasoning.*
  This also includes retentive memory.

A little exercise

Task: Write five things you know you are good at or that comes to you naturally.

This exercise should be completed before you read any further.

You may write in the space below before you continue to the next section.

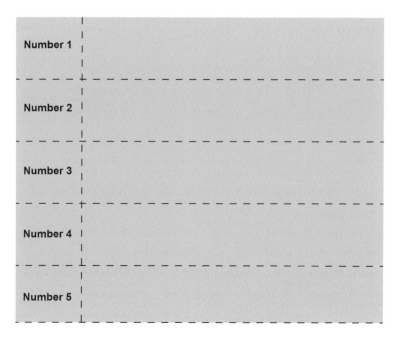

Number 1

Number 2

Number 3

Number 4

Number 5

---

*Some people have exceptional ability to reason out complex issues. It is a gift.

Talents and gifts are unique

Talents and gifts make you unique. So there is no point trying to copy someone else's gift or trying to be somebody else. Anything that you have is a gift; your height (whether short or tall), skin colour, physique and so on. Some gifts are easily discernible; others you have to consciously discover them.

What you must know about gifts or talents

- Gifts and talents are given; you are born with them (innate).
- You cannot have new gifts or talents; you can only discover them.
- Your gifts and talents are enduring and unique.
- Gifts and talents can be improved on by learning and practice.
- Improving your gifts by learning and practice develops them into strengths and abilities.
- Gifts and talents can also help you to develop useful skills.
- Your gifts can help you make better use of your time.
- It is easier to grow your talents than to improve upon your weakness.
- Your talents may sometimes be what God has designed to make you successful.
- Strangely, many people with gifts are less aware of the gifts that others see in them.

12 Pointers to gifts and talents

The following can be said about someone with identified gifts and talents:

1. Usually notices what others don't.

2. A deep thinker, most times.

3. Possession of natural abilities without formal training.

4. Tends to be a rapid or quick learner.

5. There is usually a passionate devotion to an area of gift or interest.

6. An unusual amount of energy and time may be devoted in certain situations.

7. Evidence of uncommon elaborate thoughts, ideas and imaginations.

8. Rich inner world and unusual ways of thinking to generate ideas.

9. The person approaches the world and problems differently.

10. Gifted individuals find things very easy in some areas that others struggle with.

11. The person may present results that are rare or of exceptional quality.

12. Talented people are usually gifted in more than one area.

"The definition of tragedy is to spend your entire life being someone else."
Dr Mensah Otabil

Bryce Brites (at only 20 months old!)

Bryce Brites was only 20 months old when he became the youngest professional football player on the planet. Brites was signed with Belgian club FC Racing Boxberg in November 2013 after he was invited to train with the club's Under-5 team. Brites was issued his very own Belgian FA membership card the very same day. He has been described (at that age) as someone with "highly unusual" talent and "incredible" ball control. Before him, Dutch footballer Baerke van der Meij signed a 10-year deal with VVV-Venlo when he was only 18 months old in April 2011. A clip of his 'heroic' hat-trick can be viewed on the British Broadcasting Corporation (BBC) website via the link below: http://www.bbc.co.uk/news/world-europe-13224130 .

Stephen Wiltshire MBE
(known for his retentive memory and artistic skills)

- Born in London in 1974

- Was allegedly mute and did not say a word till the age of 5

- Later said "Paper"; then, "Pen" (after a school trip), and then drew everything he saw

- Couldn't speak properly until age 9

- In 2009 – Wiltshire had a 20-minute helicopter ride over New York City

- He then made from memory an 18 feet drawing of New York skyline over three days

- Drew Empire State Building and a detailed sketch of every building was included

- Has created several famous panoramas of iconic cities around the world. Has panoramic drawings of London, New York, Tokyo, Rome, Moscow, Hong Kong, Madrid, Dubai and Jerusalem to mention a few

- He has drawn several portraits of people and other specially commissioned work

- His website at any point has more than 500 works of art and design. http://www.stephenwiltshire.co.uk/

But what did Wiltshire do to maximise his potential?

- Studied Fine Art at City & Guilds Art College, London

- Has a Master's degree in Painting, Drawing and Printmaking

- Also studied desk-top publishing and finished the course one year early!

- Stephen Wiltshire's motto is: "Do the best you can and never stop".

Aare Afe Babalola - the wonder man who specialises in private study.

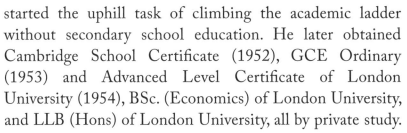

Born in 1929, Aare Afe Babalola attended Emmanuel Primary School in Ado-Ekiti in the current Ekiti State of Nigeria. In spite of his outstanding intellectual capability and offer of admission to the prestigious Christ's School, Ado-Ekiti, the opportunity of secondary school education eluded this brilliant and exceptional man due to lack of funds. He therefore started the uphill task of climbing the academic ladder without secondary school education. He later obtained Cambridge School Certificate (1952), GCE Ordinary (1953) and Advanced Level Certificate of London University (1954), BSc. (Economics) of London University, and LLB (Hons) of London University, all by private study.

Aare Afe Babalola is someone who is impressed by success and spurn on by the achievement of others and he decided to pursue a career in Law. In 1960, Afe Babalola sat for the London University Intermediate Law examination as an external candidate, and on passing that, applied for the Part 1 final examination. There was no law school in Nigeria at the time and he had to go to England. On 1 January 1961, Afe Babalola arrived in London and proceeded to register at University of London for his Law course. The Secretary to the Senate at London University who he visited told him: *"You are the wonder man who specialises in private study."* Having impressed the establishment, Afe Babalola was allowed to attend some of the lectures as a casual student. Afe Babalola found the lectures challenging because of the intensity of the English accent and also because he had become accustomed to learning privately by reading text books and making his own notes. Despite all challenges, Afe Babalola scored a double in the Bar final examinations in June and July of 1963. He became a member of Lincoln's Inn, London the same year.

Over the subsequent years, Afe Babalola became a legal luminary of repute and rose to the level of Senior Advocate of Nigeria (Nigeria's equivalent of Queen's Counsel in England). Afe Babalola's success over 50 years of legal practice distinguishes him from his peers in the legal industry. He is an astute businessman, a great leader, and a *politician* who never occupied a high profile political office. Following his sojourn as the Chancellor of the University of Lagos, Afe Babalola founded the first private university in Nigerian in 2009, and many have since followed in his footsteps. On March 11, 2015, Aare Afe Babalola became the first African to be awarded an honorary degree of Doctor of Law (LLD) by the University of London. Without any doubt, he is a man of great stature and immense ability.

Ayodeji Ayeola – Nigeria's foremost portrait artist
Ayodeji Abiodun Ayeola is the multitalented Nigerian artist who was born on April 1, 1985 to Mr Ayeola Ogunleye

and Mrs Mary Onaolapo Ayeola. Ayodeji discovered his talent early and started drawing, painting and sculpting at the age of four. He was encouraged by his parents and teachers and he later studied General Art (OND, Upper Credit) and Painting (HND, Upper Credit) at the School of Art, Design and Printing, Yaba College of Technology, Lagos, Nigeria. He is renowned for his artistic skills in life and portrait painting and has had several paintings commissioned from around the world. His portfolios include works of arts of places, ordinary people, and celebrities including entertainers, governors and presidents. Below are some of his works, which are kindly reproduced with Mr Ayeola's permission. Mr Ayeola's work can be viewed and ordered on his website at www.awizzy.net

1

*Bend down boutique' market, Lagos, Nigeria © Ayodeji Ayeola

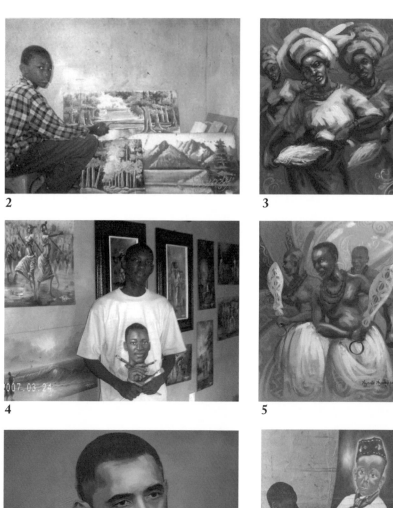

2

3

4

5

7

(2&7) Ayodeji painting at an early age (3) Dancers (4) Ayodeji in front of his works (5) Benin royal dancers (6) President Barack Obama

6

Dr Ben Carson

You may have heard about 'hand–eye coordination' and 'three-dimensional reasoning skills'. These were what Dr

Benjamin Solomon Carson said made him a gifted surgeon. Born in Detroit, Michigan to parents from rural Georgia, his parents divorced when he was 8 years old. Although initially performing at the back of his class, Carson's mother took it upon herself to make sure he and his older brother read their books. Carson later graduated from Yale University and received his M.D. from the University of Michigan Medical School. At age 33, he became the youngest major division director in Johns Hopkins history, as Director of Paediatric Neurosurgery.

Dr Ben Carson is credited with being the first surgeon to successfully separate conjoined twins joined at the head. Before then, such conjoined twins usually died during or after surgery from complications, especially exsanguination (bleeding to death). In 1987, a 50-member surgical team, led by Carson, worked for 22 hours to successfully separate the Binder conjoined twins, who had been joined at the back of the head. The twins left hospital at 14 months.

Now back to 'hand–eye coordination' and 'three-dimensional reasoning skills': to really be a good surgeon, irrespective of the advanced microscopes or the latest technology available at your disposal, your eyes must adequately see what your hand is cutting; and needless to say, your hands too must be able to cut (with finesse) what your eyes are seeing. This is especially important in heart and brain surgeries where a movement of a fraction of a millimetre can make the difference between life and death. Dr Carson was particularly gifted when it comes to coordinating his eyes and his hands when it mattered most. To Dr Carson, 'hand–eye coordination' and 'three-dimensional reasoning skills' were gifts, and he didn't do anything to deserve them. He however identified them, used them to his own advantage and the benefit of others. Ben Carson rose from a very poor and humble background to that of a world renowned neurosurgeon. Ben Carson is a household name around the world today.*

I can list here hundreds of names of people who achieved a lot through their talents, in various endeavours of life but a few here will suffice. In the music industry, you will hear of Louis Armstrong, described as one of the most successful and influential jazz musicians of all time. Others include The Beatles, Mozart, Beethoven, Elvis Prestley, Aretha Franklin, Billy Holiday, and CeCe Winans, Donnie McClurkin and Peter Smith. The world of sport features names such as Michael Jordan (basketball), Tiger Woods (Golf), Michael Phelps (Swimming), Roger Federer, Steffi Graf and the Williams' sisters – Venus and Serena (tennis), Pele (of Brazil) and Lionel Messi, Cristiano Ronaldo and David Beckham

---

*Reference: The story of Ben Carson can be read in his autobiography Gifted Hands, 1996). A good summary can also be found at http://www.biography.com/people/ben-carson-475422

(football), and Michael Schumacher (Formula 1 motor racing). In film and entertainment you will hear of Steven Spielberg, Aaron Spelling, Audrey Hepburn, Simon Fuller and Simon Cowell. All these people used their talents and became pioneers and trendsetters in their fields of endeavour.

> *"To think BIG and to use our talents doesn't mean we don't have difficulties on the way. We will - we all do. How we view those problems determines how we end up."*
> –Ben Carson

I don't want you for a moment to think that once God endowed these people with the talents, they just sat on their laurels and watched the talents and gifts grow themselves. No; not at all. These people put in endless hours of practice and dedication to reach the cutting edge of their game. For example, this is what Michael Jordan's colleagues said about him: "Even if we had just finished playing eight games that week, Michael would still go out and practice." His coach said of him: "Michael – He never takes a day off! The thing about Michael is, he takes nothing about his game for granted." The same is true for a person with musical talent and a great voice, or a man or woman that has exceptional ability to play the piano or draw or paint a masterpiece – they don't just sit and do nothing; they go to great extent to perfect their arts and to make them relevant and useful for the present time.

Make a difference

If you want to make a difference in any sphere of life you need to discover your gifts and talents. You do this by consciously thinking about them. Some call it introspection, soul searching, or even personal research. You can be extremely good at something, and it is your responsibility to find out what that something is.

So which gift is the best?

Giftings are of equal value, what distinguishes them is how much value you place on them.

What to do with your gifts
Discover the gifts.

You have to look out for the little things and consciously think about your gifts. Anytime I visited a family friend who lived nearby, their son was always drawing a house, Spiderman, Tarzan, footballers, or some unexplainable gadgets. It didn't take long for me to conclude that this boy had a gift in drawing. Fortunately his parents were aware of this and had been encouraging him to refine his skills in art.

Gifts can lay dormant for years. You have a responsibility to discover them. Consider your particular gift especially if others speak of it. Think again if other people become more interested in what you have than you are. Where you are today is not your best. Look inside, and try to identify your strongest tendencies and inclinations. Your gifts and talents might just lie therein.

Develop your gifts

Many times talents and gifts are in raw form. Find it, refine it, study it and validate it. It may not be perfect now, let it develop. Cultivate and build your gifts. Your gift is what gives you a unique identity that sets you apart from others.

In order to develop your gifts you have to adopt the 3P-approach. Once you have your 3Ps aligned, you have to study more, research, practice, and practice again. Now the 3Ps:

- **Purpose.** What is the purpose of your gift? Find the right use for them. Mainly it would be to add value to the lives of others and to bring positive change.

- **People.** You must associate with the right people who will help you to maximise your gifts and talents. These people may help in one capacity or the other – to give advice, direct, support, birth, refine, defend, promote and celebrate your gifts. We all need people in our lives, and there is nothing such as a 'self-made' man. Find a mentor if you want to go where you have never been before.

- **Place.** For your gift to blossom, you have to be in the right place and environment. This is one of the secrets of success of many of the businesses start-ups that grew out of the Silicon Valley. Facebook is one of them. The environment of the Silicon Valley encourages collaboration between universities and industry and provides multiple support services that enable new companies and their ideas to grow and flourish without feeling threatened or overwhelmed.

It is however important to get into the right place. If you have artistic talents, find your way to galleries or art fairs and not swimming pools; of course only if you are at the pool to rest after work or to be inspired.

Please avoid dream-killers and time wasters*. By this I mean:

- People that say everything is not possible. You might hear from those people: "It's not going to work."

- Negative people who are always negative about everything.

- Bad company who want to pull you away from your dreams.

- People who want to chat with you even though they know you are busy at your work or assignment.

Deploy your gifts and talents

Gifts must be used in appropriate places and situations. The gift you don't use will soon be lost. Every divine deposit multiplies with use. You must use your *gift muscle* for profit, for learning, for understanding better and for passing your skills to the next generation.

*See 12 examples of time-wasting under 'Time' on page 128

"Most people unfortunately do not push themselves to excel and the problem is not a lack of capacity. Over a period of 20 years I have observed many talented students who squander their gifts. It is not ability that is missing. It is will." - Andrew Bernstein

CAVEATS

Gifts will never develop themselves. No matter how blessed, without preparation your gifting will be wasted. Associating with the wrong people may ruin opportunities or wreck your career no matter how gifted you are. Gifts can kill when they are not properly controlled or channelled.

3 Things I Will Do Today

- Make a list of my gifts and talents and narrow down to five of them.

- Decide which one of my gifts could meet my current greatest need.

- Utilise that gift for a purpose to achieve a desired outcome.

Chapter 5

O
Opportunities

Opportunities

Definition: A time or set of circumstances that makes it possible to do something.

No matter what your IQ is or your level of education, the career pathway you follow, the people you employ or the men and women that surround you, you need opportunity, time and chance for things to happen in your life. The problem however is that opportunity, time and chance don't often announce themselves. Even when they arrive, these factors don't announce: "We are here."

You may have heard before: "Look around you; there are opportunities everywhere!" That certainly might be true in most cases, but unless you are conscious of it, you will not be aware. Being conscious demands being deliberate and being prepared, and this take effort. When opportunity comes, it will be too late to begin to prepare; and opportunity may be lost and never regained. That is why you have to 'live ready' and seize the moment. When opportunity meets preparation, success is inevitable. If you miss the preparation stage, opportunities will elude you.

One Pound Fish

Muhammad Shahid Nazir also known as the 'One Pound Fish Man' is a Pakistani trader and recording artist who found fame as an internet sensation for his viral video,

'One Pound Fish'. Nazir was born in the town of Pattoki, near Lahore in Punjab, Pakistan. He grew up listening to Bollywood* and Punjabi music and worked for the family-owned transport company prior to moving to the UK. He worked in the UK briefly at a pound shop. He later began work on a fish stall at Queen's Market, Upton Park, east London where he used to attract customers using a trader's call. He soon composed the song, 'One Pound Fish' with the lyrics:

Come on ladies, come on ladies
One pound fish
Have-a, have-a look
One pound fish
Very, very good, very, very cheap
One pound fish
Six for five pound
One pound each

Muhammad Shahid Nazir's simple song became an internet hit and a viral video allegedly after members of the public passing by his market stall uploaded videos of Nazir performing his song onto YouTube. He later appeared in the UK edition of the X Factor and was signed by Warner Music as a recording artist in November 2012. He has since released videos of his song with various artists. 'One Pound Fish', a song that started from a market stall has even been covered by artists including Alesha Dixon and Timbaland. If you have ever seen the One Pound Fish video on YouTube,

Bollywood is the Hindi-Language film industry based in Mumbai (Bombay), Maharashtra, India you will agree that anything can be a gift or talent. But for me that was more of an opportunity than a talent or gift. It was also an opportunity that Nazir grabbed with both hands.

David Beckham (again!)

On 17 August 1996, the first day of the Premier League season, David Beckham, in a 'Number 10' shirt, became something of a household name after he scored a spectacular goal in a match against Wimbledon FC. With Manchester United FC leading 2–0, Beckham noticed that Wimbledon's goalkeeper, Neil Sullivan, was standing a long way out of his goal post. Beckham then hit a shot from the halfway line that floated over the goalkeeper's head and into the net. Beckham grabbed that opportunity and that made a big difference to his career. This is how Beckham puts it in his own words:

"It changed my life. The ball seemed to be in the air for hours and it all went quiet. Then the ball went in and it just erupted. I was on cloud nine. I just wanted to shake everybody's hand and be out on the pitch for an hour."

Beckham, no doubt, is a man of skills and talents; but on many occasions he took advantage of the opportunities that life presented to him – in football, business and advertising. But if he had not prepared himself to act skilfully when those diverse opportunities showed up, the chances would have eluded him, forever.

7 kinds of opportunities and what to do with them

1. Opportunities that you possess – cherish them.

2. Opportunities given to you – utilise them in time.

3. Opportunities that you stumble upon – take advantage of them.

4. Opportunities you are looking for – be optimistic and patient.

5. Opportunities that are looking for you – discern them.

6. Opportunities that you see in others – position yourself.

7. Opportunities that you create – be strategic and precise.

The opportunity of a lifetime must be seized within the lifetime of the opportunity.

Leonard Ravenhill (1907–1994)

THE 7 LEVELS OF OPPORTUNITIES

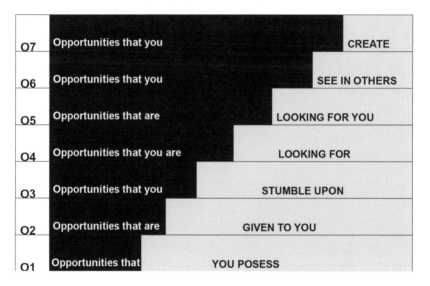

O7	Opportunities that you	CREATE
O6	Opportunities that you	SEE IN OTHERS
O5	Opportunities that are	LOOKING FOR YOU
O4	Opportunities that you are	LOOKING FOR
O3	Opportunities that you	STUMBLE UPON
O2	Opportunities that are	GIVEN TO YOU
O1	Opportunities that	YOU POSESS

The above opportunities can be ranked in order of your being in control and their ability to give maximum results.

O1- OPPORTUNITIES THAT YOU POSSESS

If you are endowed or possess any tangible or intangible attributes, cherish them and be grateful as you did not do anything to deserve or possess them. It may be that you are born into a wealthy family, a prosperous nation or with a gift of the voice of an angel or dancing or wisdom or any other thing for that matter. Cherish them, use them for positive actions and don't let them go to waste.

O2- OPPORTUNITIES GIVEN TO YOU

Every day of life, men and women, boys and girls, are given opportunities to be or to do something; it is important that those opportunities are not taken for granted. Such opportunities should be utilised in good time to improve self and others, and to make positive impact. Otherwise the opportunities may be passed on to others who are willing to make use of them. When you are given an opportunity, time is of essence. Your benefactor will not wait forever and time will not stop for you to get ready.

I have been fortunate to live in two different parts of the world – one in a developing country where opportunities are so limited due to political instability, corruption and mismanagement of national resources, and the other, in a highly developed country where opportunities abound. What sometimes strikes me in the developed country is how a lot of people, particularly young adults, throw away opportunities for funded education, vocational training and job prospects. Indeed they allow themselves to get distracted and side-tracked by indiscipline, complacency and lack of focus which is not helped by the media (TV, billboards, magazines and the internet) peddling fame, lust, sex and an unhealthy sense of entitlement. When I have the opportunity, I say to such young people: "Get real; make hay when the sun is shining. You are not going to be young forever!"

03 - OPPORTUNITIES THAT YOU STUMBLE UPON

If you stumble upon a good (and relevant) opportunity, take advantage of it. Grab it; don't let it go. There may be need for you to negotiate and partner with others, upgrade yourself by learning and up skilling in other to maximally take advantage of the opportunity that you stumble upon. If you happen to stumble upon gold or oil in your back yard (it doesn't happen every day), that is not the time for you to say you are not a 'gold-digger' or that you are an environmentalist or that you'll rather wait and see. Some clever people may ask to buy your house or garden and then take possession of the resources. Don't be silly or play ignorance. One of my associates, Karis Kolawole, a consultant and coach, gave me this advice: 'Even if you feel not ready, think of what you can do to be able to make use of the opportunity.'

04- OPPORTUNITIES THAT YOU ARE LOOKING FOR

You will need to be proactive, optimistic and patient if you are looking for certain opportunities. I meet people from time to time who say they are 'looking for an opportunity' for one thing or the other. I have been in that position a few times myself – for example when I was 'looking for an opportunity' to come to England or to buy a house in a particular area or to meet a prospective customer or client. Having good mentors have however taught me that even while you are 'looking for an opportunity', you really have to be prepared. You don't just sit and do nothing! It goes without saying that if you are looking for good friendship, you also show yourself as friendly to others and not just go and sit (or hide) in a bunker. In the same way, if you are looking to land a business contract or deal, you have to put yourself forward, and let prospective customers know what you are selling and why they should buy from you. The truth is this: many hundreds (or thousands) are looking for the same kind of opportunities, all over the world. So, you have to invest in what you are looking for.

05- OPPORTUNITIES THAT ARE LOOKING FOR YOU

Discernment is key when it comes to an opportunity or opportunities that are looking for you. You have to discern them. When IBM wanted to improve their computer sales, they needed a better processor to install on their machines. At the time, the company that later grew into the giant Microsoft had the MS-DOS software. IBM reached a deal with Bill Gates, but did not purchase exclusive right for MS-DOS to be used only on their machines. So Mr Gates was able to sell to other computer manufacturers who installed MS-DOS on their machines. The MS-DOS software made Microsoft a lot of money, and to me, the opportunity was out there looking for Microsoft, and found them. But note this: when an opportunity is looking for you, you have to have something to offer.

I was told the story of a young woman who studied Chemistry at the university. During her national service, she was posted to the northern part of Nigeria where the only thing on offer for her was to teach Maths and Science at a local primary school. She was lucky if half of her class of 23 pupils showed up at lessons. She was bored and eagerly awaited the end of that service year. But in the meantime she would regularly visit the nearby market where local women and men made beautiful designs (embroidery) on clothes with needles and thread. In no time, she mastered how to make colourful designs and also learnt how to sew clothes–something she did just to mark the time.

When this graduate of Chemistry eventually left for Canada to join her husband, she learnt that when women in her Nigerian community there wanted specially designed attires for special occasions, they either had to import their dresses from Nigeria or order from an African-American shop in Chicago, Illinois. Both were at an exorbitant cost without quality or perfect fit being guaranteed! One of the women noticed this graduate always dressed herself and her family gorgeously for special celebrations and asked her where she got her attires from. The lady informed the woman that she sewed the clothes and made the designs herself. News soon spread around the African community that traditional attires could now be made locally by one of their own. That was the beginning of a cloth-making business for the Chemistry graduate who turned her garage into a sewing mistress shop. Today her business has expanded beyond Canada and she is now serving hundreds of customers across North America. Essentially, that opportunity was looking for her, and she did not waste time when she stumbled upon it.

06- OPPORTUNITIES THAT YOU SEE IN OTHERS

If you see an opportunity in another person, don't be shy or timid about exploring it. Position yourself and find the common good. If you don't, others will take advantage of the same opportunity. The most important thing is to look for how the opportunity will benefit you and the other person. I once met a lady with excellent typing and administrative skills. She could also write and speaks very good English. Her challenge was her inability to organise herself and put all her ideas on paper in order to package them. That was what I was good at and I could help her publish her materials, so that was what I did. That opportunity also benefited me as I desperately needed somebody who could quickly type up several ideas that were in my head. The association benefited both of us but it was because I spotted the opportunity first.

07- OPPORTUNITIES THAT YOU CREATE

This is the highest level of opportunity that anyone could have – when you create one. But you must be careful to be strategic and definite in what you are creating, otherwise you could waste a lot of time and effort. The opportunity that you create must necessarily meet a need. And you have to be strategic and precise. Wise people create opportunities instead of waiting to meet some. The best way to prepare for an opportunity is by creating it. Ask yourself some serious questions: have you spotted something, or have you noticed something strange today? What have you done about it?

One of the most beneficial ways of creating opportunities for yourself is to go and help people or to study at the *University of Life* in whatever country you may live. I started teaching as a small boy of 8 or 9. When I visited a friend early one Saturday morning, my friend's mother, who was the teacher at the extra-tuition classes holding in her house, had quickly stepped out to purchase some food items. When she returned, to her surprise, her noisy students who were much younger than me were totally taken in by my almost theatrical way of teaching A-B-C. I was offered a job there and then, and was paid the equivalent of 10 pence every week.

Also, when I was in secondary school, I would hand-copy my class notes for few of my classmates who were too busy to write notes in class. I was paid for my service, and at the same time revised for the exams as I wrote the notes all over again. The results were predictable: I passed, but some of those classmates did not do too well.

Again, when I was in medical school, I taught some of the junior classes Biochemistry; and, when I later produced 'Bioquiz' - a Biochemistry hand-out for sale, I did not require any advertisement. I did not set out to sell revision materials and I only taught the junior classes because teaching was just a part of me. But, I saw a gap and maximized the opportunity.

Finally, in 2001 after I completed my professional examinations in Psychiatry, I compiled all the materials I had used for one of the practicals (a somewhat unpredictable and difficult components of the exam) and used them to train others. Using the same materials, I later invited another colleague of mine to co-write a revision book titled, *Patient Management Problems in Psychiatry* (published by Elsevier Science, 2005). The book was not a bestseller by any account but by the time sales went down after the exam formats were changed, I and my colleague had been paid over £5,000 in royalties.

Be a man or woman of wisdom – create opportunities

Each of the above categories of opportunities must be approached differently. According to an adage that has been variously credited to the American inventor Thomas Edison and other writers, "The reason most people do not recognize an opportunity when they meet it, is because it usually goes around wearing overalls and looking like hard work." It is however important to recognise these opportunities for what they are. Opportunities are like windows – they don't stay open forever. You must be prepared for every opportunity that you expect or the one that may come your way.

Wise people don't wait for opportunities; they create them. These people look for where to invest their resources and pursue their dreams passionately. Success is one per cent the idea and 99 per cent the execution. Don't wait for things to be perfect, begin to work on what you have. It took me a while to learn this lesson, and you must learn quicker than I did.

How to spot an opportunity

- Keep your eyes open.
- Act fast. Where there is a problem, a challenge or a need, there is an opportunity.
- Ask the right questions: "Is there a need here? Can I make it better or faster or less expensive?"
- Embrace what you are not used to; something great

might just be close by.

- Check the trends, think and focus.
- If someone knocks your idea off the perch, thank them instead of arguing.
- Consider every suggestion; you don't have to accept them.

NO NEWS IS GOOD NEWS

A journalist was sent to cover the opening of a brand new hospital in a rural part of Nigeria in the early 1980s. The event, costing about 300,000 Naira (over USD $250,000 at the time) was scheduled to be opened by the state governor; and several dignitaries from nearby states had been invited. The reporter mingled with some of the guests who were being served refreshments while they waited for the governor's arrival. Suddenly, the reporter noticed that the seats were gradually becoming empty and people had been leaving. There was a big canopy with capacity to seat 2,000 guests; and there was no rain or thunderstorm. So why were people leaving?

The event had been cancelled as the state governor had taken ill. The reporter was dejected and returned to his TV station to tell his boss that there was no news coverage due to the cancellation. The reporter expected his boss to be disappointed but to his surprise, the news editor wasn't shocked or furious at all. The editor asked: "What do you mean there is no news story? You mean an event costing that huge amount of public money with guests from all over the country was cancelled just like that? Why can't they send in the deputy governor or one of the commissioners? Why keep the hospital locked for another one month while the governor recovered? This is even a bigger story, and the public would like to know." The editor was right; the story caused a big stir during the prime time evening slot. Where the journalist saw disappointment, his news editor saw a great opportunity.

Ways to maximise opportunities

1. Consider the seven levels of opportunities on page 55. Discern which ones pertain to you.

2. Consciously think about opportunities; they are everywhere and are waiting to be grabbed.

3. Constantly look out for opportunities – sometimes they are like a moving cloud – they don't stay in the same position for ever.

4. Be sensitive to opportunities – they can come disguised as responsibilities. Also be careful; some are traps and not worth it.

5. Look for ways to maximise the opportunities.

6. Guard any opportunity that you have jealously and don't let them go to waste.

7. Ask which opportunity has the greatest chance of success. Don't waste time on what appears to

be a good opportunity but yields very low return for your time and effort or investment.

8. Do something about the opportunities that present themselves to you. Don't think an idea to death or wait for when everything is going to be perfect.

9. Never give up. If anything is proving too hard to crack, know that others might be feeling the same way too. You will certainly be at an advantage if you get there first. Also, seek help.

10. Learn from mistakes, particularly if you have missed an opportunity. Almost always, another opportunity is around the corner.

12 reasons why people miss or misuse opportunities

- Failure to recognize opportunities.

- Lack of ambition, goals or targets.

- Lack of preparation, capability and capacity.

- Fear of failure, adverse consequences or of suffering.

- Concerns about being embarrassed, ridiculed or rejected.

- The comfort of the 'comfort zone' and the lure of the familiar.

- Easier or easy alternatives, perfectionism and waiting for the ideal time.

- Negative mindset and focus on short-term gain.

- Lack of passion and self-confidence, and mistrust.

- Procrastination, complacency or laziness.

- Other people's opinion and distractions. "What will people say?"

- Obstructive or hostile environment.

"Nothing can change the past; we can only learn from it. If at any point in your life you miss an opportunity, ponder only for a little while and move on. When one door closes, another door opens. But we often look so long and regretfully upon the closed door, that we do not see the ones which open almost instantly for us, as that door closes."
- Alexander Graham Bell – inventor of the telephone.

BE CAREFUL OF 'QUICK FIXES'

Opportunities are important but you must be careful about certain opportunities that promise quick gain, overnight or instant success without much effort or investment of time and resources. If an opportunity appears too good to be true, it is most likely it is.

3 Things I Will Do Today

1. Consider which of the seven opportunities I have now.

2. Decide how I will make use of the opportunity.

3. Find one thing I can use the opportunity for today.

Chapter 7

A
Abilities

Abilities

Definition: Ability is defined as the possession of the qualities required to do something.

Abilities have to do with the capability of being able to do something or carry out a function or task, time and time again - with measurable, predictable and reproducible and satisfactory outcomes. You need to have ability, strength and wisdom to hold your own. You need strength if you are going to rise to higher ground. You need strength to strategise and operate in any area of life if you are not to be left behind or forgotten. Many times this does not refer only to physical strength or practical [which has to do with performance] abilities which are described in the chapter titled Skills. You must however know that you have all it takes to get the best out of life - if only you will do something with it!

Below are examples of people with abilities and strengths

Baroness Tanni Grey-Thompson, DBE

Born on 26 July 1969 with spina bifida*, Dame Tanni Grey-Thompson is a formidable personality who refused to allow her being differently abled limit her ability to achieve.

---

*Spina bifida is a birth defect where there is incomplete closing of the backbone and membranes around the spinal cord.

She is a former British wheelchair racer, a television presenter and a parliamentarian who was appointed to the UK House of Lords in March 2010. Over her career she won a total of 16 Paralympic medals, including 11 golds, 13 World Championship medals (six gold, five silver and two bronze).

Winston Churchill

This British former Prime Minister and statesman is well known for his abilities as a great leader, speaker, Army officer, a historical writer, and an artist. Churchill's ability to rally a nation during the Second World War has been cited as a major decisive factor in the winning of the war.

Thomas Edison

Thomas Edison was a man who did not know how to give up and someone who was well known for his creativity and inventions. Edison created many appliances (long lasting light bulb, phonograph and over 1000 other products) that have changed the world forever.

Dr David Oyedepo

Born in Oshogbo in south west of Nigeria, Dr (Bishop) David Olaniyi Oyedepo is popularly known for his exploits in Christian ministry. Dr David Oyedepo, through divine guidance grew a church of four people to a mega church of multiple millions of members across the globe. A man with a sharp mind and tireless work ethic, Dr David Oyedepo received a Ph.D. in Human Development from Honolulu University, Hawaii, United States. Under his able leadership and divine guidance, the Faith Tabernacle, a 50,000 seat church auditorium (largest in the world: the Guinness Book of Records) was constructed within less than 12 months. Dr Oyedepo's distinct abilities are in staying focused on what he believes and thinks is important, avoiding distractions and raising leaders. Today, Dr Oyedepo ranks among the giants in Christian ministry and church growth with the likes of Dr David Yonggi Cho (formerly Paul Yungi Cho) of South Korea.

The Williams Sisters

The older Venus Williams and younger Serena Williams are both American professional tennis players of immense ability and strength. Venus, as of 2015 was a seven-time Grand Slam title winner (singles) while Serena has bagged 21 Grand Slam titles. Their immense abilities were discovered at an early age and cultivated and improved upon by their father who is also their coach.

Srinivasa Ramanujan (1887 -1920)

Ramanujan was known for his natural ability to master Mathematics. He mastered a complete maths book (*Advanced Trigonometry* by S. L. Loney) by the age of 13, and even discovered theorems of his own. A man credited with sharp memory, calculative mind, patience and insight, Ramanujan compiled nearly 4,000 equations* and identities (equation that is true no matter what values are chosen) before he [tragically] died at the age of 32 years.

Working at a job that you love is likely to make you happier, more enthusiastic and earn you more money.

Ellen Johnson Sirleaf

The first female national president in the continent of Africa has been described as a woman of exceptional ability. Sirleaf survived a violent marriage, single

*Nearly all of Ramanujan's works and claims have now been proven correct.

motherhood, poverty, a coup d'état, imprisonment and civil wars. An accomplished author and champion of Women's Rights, she also worked as an economist at the World Bank before being elected to lead the nation of Liberia in 2006. By her positioning, Sirleaf has joined the league of influential women such as the former Indian president, Indira Gandhi, former British Prime Minister, late Margaret Thatcher and Angela Merkel of Germany.

Indira Gandhi

Indira Gandhi was the third President of India. Although a controversial figure, Indira Gandhi's abilities and strength stemmed from her toughness and skilled political manoeuvrings. Assassinated on October 31 1984, Indira Gandhi was a woman respected by her friends and foes.

Warren Buffett

Warren Buffett, also popularly known as the 'Sage of Omaha' has been described as the most successful investor of the 20th century. He has many things going for him: ability to see which good investment to trade in and which stock to buy; ability to know when to buy and when to sell; ability to know who to partner with and when to call off unproductive ventures and relationships; ability to accept defeat and to own up when things are not working as expected; and ability in cutting short his losses. One of the sage's many abilities and strengths not commonly spoken of is his ability to keep his feet firmly on the ground despite his stupendous and extraordinary wealth. It is widely reported that Mr Buffett has mainly lived in the same house and in the same neighbourhood for over 50 years!

Demis Hassabis

Demis Hassabis is a British Artificial Intelligence* (AI) researcher who has several abilities in different fields. He is gifted in many areas but Hassabis is a good example of someone who has been able to deploy his abilities and strengths in varying fields. Born in 1976, and a child prodigy in chess, Hassabis reached the masters standard at the age of 13. Once rated the second best  chess player in the world, he finished his A-Levels two years earlier and started developing computer games at the age of 16. He studied computer science at Cambridge University, ran businesses for several years and then pursued a PhD in Cognitive Neuroscience at the University College London. In 2011, he co-founded DeepMind Technologies, a London-based machine-learning start-up. DeepMind Technologies was later acquired by Google for a reported £400 million in January 2014.

*The theory and development of computer systems able to perform tasks normally requiring human intelligence, such as visual perception, speech recognition, decision-making and translation between languages. So when you speak a name into your computer and it starts to call the person, that is Artificial Intelligence at work.

What about you and me?

The attentive reader would have noticed in the examples given above that the various abilities differ in their qualities and what they are used for. It is important to know what your abilities are because if you don't, you will be drawn or dragged into certain areas that either look impressive or promising. Mostly what may put you under pressure to be what you are not, are things that have the tendency to feed your ego. Am I suggesting that you should not stretch yourself or become a better person? Big 'NO'. But, you must realise that anytime you are operating outside of your of giftings and abilities, it will be a constant and perpetual struggle. Don't let that be you! Instead, stay focused on what you are good at and let this be followed by peace in your heart. Get to know who you are because you cannot afford to live your life being someone else.

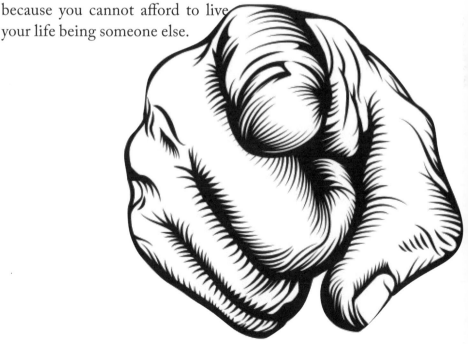

When it comes to abilities and strength, you must do seven things:

Identify areas of your strength

Ask yourself before you ask others what you are good at. Don't despise what you have even though it might look like nothing now.

Speak passionately about it

People don't know about what you don't speak about. This is the main reason why Coca-Cola Company and Apple Inc. (the manufacturer of iPods, iPhones, iPads tablets and Apple Mac computers) still advertise their very successful products. Speak about what you have. You never know who may be listening.

Build up or develop your strength

Any muscle that is not exercised will soon go weak. Whatever you can do now, you can do better. Develop yourself by reading, studying, and go for mentoring and coaching to get help.

Look for practical ways to deploy your ability and strength

If you have strengths in particular area, use them to benefit others or move a cause forward. Don't always wait to be asked. If you have been at a role in your job, volunteer when other challenges come up. Ask for new opportunities at your place of employment.

Operate mainly in the area of your strength

The greatest investment you can ever make is in yourself. You must regularly evaluate your strengths and weaknesses. Don't aim to be good at everything; become very good in the areas you enjoy most. This is further discussed in detail below.

Use your strength to cause positive change

The essence of any form of ability or strength is to promote positive change; otherwise strength and abilities will be for show or for destruction.

Balance your abilities and strength with humility

Many people in the world today have abilities and strengths which have never been tapped into due to lack of opportunities or chance. So if you have been given opportunity to use what you have, be grateful and at the same time humble. Never let it get to your head.

Questions to help you identify your abilities and areas of strength

- What do you most enjoy doing?
- What have you been very good at doing in the past?
- What would be your ideal job? It doesn't matter what it is.
- What areas have you achieved the best results in previously?
- What ideas or tasks come easy to you?

- If you had all the money and time, what would you spend it on?

- What one thing would you do even if you were not paid for it?

- What areas have other people said that you have been most helpful?

- What endeavours give you the most satisfaction or pleasure?

What and where do you derive abilities and strength from?

- Your God-given gifts, talents and endowment.

- What you are born with (genetic factors) such as your intellect, height or physique.

- Your background and environment.

- Your character and disposition.

- Interests, inclinations and keen observations.

- Experiences – positive and negative.

- Education, training and mentoring.

- Your achievements, successes, failures and disappointments.

- Your associations, interests, and affiliations.

- Your stance (what you are persuaded of).

- Teaching and training of others.

Strength, Attitude and Character

Whether you call them strengths, attitudes or character, you should develop and deploy your attributes to make them work for you. Think, and consciously think about these things, and you will see you have a lot going for you. The following will make you stand out in any endeavour of life:

Strength

The strength of a person helps them to function at their best and to achieve results. This could be, for example, ability to lead, hardwork, patience, being self-motivated, quick learner, friendly, very practical, good communication skills, good listener, smart worker, team player, adaptability and good humour. The good thing about strengths is that they can be acquired and developed.

Attitude

A positive attitude, punctuality, being happy to help, being sincere, dedicated, enthusiastic, optimistic, reliable, dependable, honest and loyal, self-confident, humble, respectful, and self-belief will serve you well always.

Character

Character is moral force or integrity and a combination of traits and qualities that distinguishes a person. The word "character" comes from a Greek word spelt as "karakter". When a craftsman makes his product, he puts his trademark (or insignia or signature) on it; so when you see a product, whether a moulded brick or shoe, you look for the signature of the maker. By the insignia on the product, you know who made it. The same is true of character – what you produce expresses who you are. In one of his teachings, Dr Tayo Adeyemi of blessed memory said: "Your work is a reflection and an extension of your character; if you are a sloppy person, your work will be sloppy; if you are a lazy person your work will be lazy; if you are a second class person your work will be second class and if you are a careless person your work will be careless." And nobody wants to hang around a lazy, careless or second class person. That got me thinking: talents may take you to the top but only character will keep you there!

How to Develop Your Abilities and Strengths

You can do anything if you set your mind to it; you just have to discover and develop your strengths. If you want to learn how to do a task, the first thing to do is to make up your mind and decide! But make sure it is something you will enjoy doing. Look for opportunities where you can learn on a job through vocation, volunteering or just by helping out. Study manuals, take extra courses in your own time, buy books, watch videos and listen to audios on your subject and what you want to do. Spend quality time talking to trusted people who are already doing what you are trying to do. Some people refer to this as 'networking.' Try and work with what has worked well for others in your field. Many times, it is not necessary to re-invent the wheel. I call it 'modelling the masters'.

It Worked for Me

When I first started publishing books (something that has long been a passion), I knew I would be relying on a lot of the abilities I already use in my daytime job as a medical doctor and a forensic psychiatrist – assessing complex situations, reading, reviewing, writing, editing, proofreading reports, and giving opinions. I had prepared a handout in Biochemistry when I was at medical school. I already co-authored a professional book *Patient Management Problems in Psychiatry* for postgraduate doctors which was published by Elsevier Science in 2005. The latter gave me a lot of experience of the challenges that authors face. I also had a few publications in local and international psychiatric journals. But, I knew I had to do more. So I started by looking at a few major self-publishers to see what they were doing.

I was also working on the manuscript for my book *Destiny Hidden in Dark Places* at the time so I used it as the guinea pig. One of my good friends and associate, Alex Iwuoha, was publishing a newspaper at the time, and he kindly published some of my articles. I asked Alex to give me some voluntary editing and proofreading jobs to do and he obliged. I also **volunteered** as a key member of a group that published weekly and quarterly magazines at my local church, which gave me more **opportunities to do** what I loved doing and have always wanted to do. I was learning too. I further learnt how the publishing industry works, and to a large extent gained **knowledge** about the 'ins and outs' of book publishing without spending too   much money. I made some valuable

contacts and money in the process. I later published a book for one of the contacts I had met through Alex and I used the **opportunity** to learn from my **mistakes** without getting my fingers burnt. Actually, I had one finger *burnt* some time ago – I said too much to a client who then went to publish her book elsewhere, but I **learnt** a lesson.

You may start to wonder where I got the time to do all of this even though I was employed in a challenging full-time job. I used my weekends and holidays. I offered to help after working hours and at weekends. I spent some of my holidays shadowing people in the industry. I also went on a 10-week InDesign book formatting **training**, not to become a graphic designer, but to communicate better with designers and book formatters that I work with. In addition, I helped with publications for several special events, workshops and conferences.

Now, I want you to go back and check the key words and phrases highlighted in bold again – decide, look for opportunities, study, courses, networking, modelling, jobs to do, volunteered, learnt, knowledge, contacts, learnt from my mistakes, offered to help, shadowing, and training. These are what improved my abilities; there was no short cut. I had to pay the price!

Energy and Passion

If you want to operate in areas where you require ability and strength, you must focus on what gives you energy. Stop working on projects that bring you down or drain life out of you. If you have to force yourself to do something that is not working, stop; it is not for you. Instead, look for things that you actually enjoy. When there is no longer passion in what you do, everybody suffers. You suffer, your clients won't be happy; the people that you work with won't be as productive. Your friends, family and associates will soon find out that you are not performing at your very best. And guess what? You might end up becoming a grumpy old man or woman.

Operating mainly in the area of strength

I knew long time ago I was never going to make it big in comedy or make a living telling jokes; and this has been confirmed by my three children. I stopped telling jokes some time ago, and lately, I have heard less of '*Daddy…that was a very dry joke!*'

The writing and the images on page 86 show what happens when people operate in areas of strength and also in areas where they are less able. The difference is clear and drives home the message. Try and write clearly with your dominant and non-dominant hands and note how you feel while engaging in the act and the quality of the output you produced.

Never mistake ability or (activity) for productivity. You may be active doing a particular task, but not really producing much when you are operating outside your areas of strength.

Right-handed 31 year-old graduate

Writing using Right Hand	Writing using Left Hand
I am a nurse and I love what I do because it makes people happy HRE	I am a nurse and I love what I do because it makes people happy HRE

Right-handed 10 year-old pupil

Drawing using Right Hand	Drawing using Left Hand

10 results of not operating in your area of strength

1. Unsteady – people make mistakes; natural or smooth course not followed.

2. Untidy – work that is produced is rough and not appealing to the eyes.

3. Illegible – people cannot really read or appreciate what you are writing.

4. Painful – quite obvious in most situations. If you are a right (or left)-handed person, try and use the opposite hand to write a short essay or draw a masterpiece on canvas.

5. Uncomfortable – that speaks for itself, and it causes stress. Try and write your signature on a piece of paper with your non-dominant (not preferred) hand to see how it feels.

6. Time wasting – days and weeks are spent on what should have taken hours.

7. Slanted – task not properly aligned, and is easily moved out of space.

8. Bodily adjustment – you have to stretch yourself, bend, or crouch over.

9. Blame game – tendency is to find someone else to

blame when the expected result is not achieved.

10. Unappreciated – No matter what you do, people don't appreciate it.

CAVEATS

Ability might get you to the top but only character will keep you there.

3 Things I Will Do Today

1. Write down the names of five people of specific abilities that I know and find out exactly what makes them tick.

2. Critically think about one or two challenges that I have today and write it (them) down.

3. Determine what ability or strength is required to bring about a solution or make improvement. The strength might actually be to be realistic and ask for help.

Chapter 8

S
Skills

"You don't always think something is a skill until you actually do it"

- **Chelsea Harmer**

Skills

Definition: A skill is defined as the ability to do something well; an expertise.

We live in a world of skills; a place where winners sometimes take all. So for the New World, skills = possibilities. What skills am I referring to then? There are mainly three types:

- Job related skills (JRS) or Specialist skills (SS)
- Transferable skills (TS)
- Self-management skills (SMS)

This is the formula for Skills: JRS (or SS) + TS + SMS = Possibilities.

It is not enough to just have one set of skills; you should have the combination of this skill sets in order to perform well at your job. Of what use is a good doctor with excellent surgical skill [positive (+ve) SS] who cannot work well with nurses or the anaesthetist in an operating theatre [lacking in TS] or who keeps cancelling appointments because he was always late [lacking in SMS]? Or, how would you like to support a football team whose excellent captain [positive (+ve) JRS/SS] kept being sent off (after being shown red cards) for abusing the referee [lacking in SMS]?

JOB RELATED SKILLS

These are the skills people use to do their job. Job related skills will keep you in a job, but that is until a robot or a computer is employed to take your place. The table on the next page will help you to identify many of the job skills that you may have but which may remain dormant or hidden until you do something about them.

The list is endless, and it includes many skills that you may not even have thought of. Do you know that people pay others to walk their dogs, groom their pets, organise parties for animals, and also (wait for this), to take their animals on holiday? There is something called 'animal hotels', for example, a cattery or a dog house. Surprised? You don't have to be! How else do you expect very rich people to spend their money? Someone dreamt up these ideas and offered the service to the people that have the money to pay for it.

EXAMPLES OF JOB RELATED SKILLS		
Practical	**Technical**	**Service**
Cooking, acting, Child care	Editing, Proofreading	Supervision, mentoring, mediation
Transcribing, typing, artwork	Gardening, horticultural work, landscaping	Public relations, advertising, image making, lobbying
Driving (forklift), horse riding, motor racing	Surveying, spying, investigation and research	Planning, organising, project management
Hairdressing, barbering, make up / beauty therapist or consultant	Electrical wiring, networking, installation	Speaking, lecturing, telephoning, telesales
Sewing, bridal services	Architectural designs, web designs	Delivery, transport, haulage
Design, construction work, bricklaying, dismantling	Computer networking and repairs	Record /Book keeping
Auto, tyre and general electrical repairs	Neurosurgery, oil drilling	Ordering, purchasing, supply
Dog or cat grooming, pet care	Accountancy, audit, data analysis	Financial services, banking, accounting, insurance
Mechanics, carpentry	Software and games, e-learning development	Consulting, training, managing
Cleaning, plumbing	Piloting, navigation, deep sea diving, space exploration	Representing, deputising
Sports, entertaining, composing	Engineering	Media review
Policing, soldiering	Film making	Directing, observing

Sir Alex Ferguson

Many people in the world today would have heard or read about Sir Alex Ferguson, the former Manchester United Football Club (FC) manager who retired in May 2013 after a 26-year stint at the helm of affairs at the club. He is a highly talented man and one with immense skills. His skills are what gave him relevance. Some of his skills are enumerated below.

Skills for a football coach like Sir Alex Ferguson

- Should be able to play the game well. Alex Ferguson was a talented footballer in his days.
- Ability to effectively coach players.
- Understand the technical skills needed to succeed.
- Ability to supervise young and mature adults (including very rich players).
- Ability to understand the value of observing.
- The ability to see especially what is unexpected.
- The ability to make decisions (instant and crucial).
- Skills in getting on with people (employers, players and fans).
- Ability to control emotions and not get sent off all the time.

- Adaptation skills, including calculated risk taking–when it matters most.

- Team forming and team building through motivation and behavioural modelling.

Apart from some technicalities involved in the game of football, the skills deployed by Sir Alex Ferguson during his coaching career apply to most managers today. Ferguson combined excellent job related skills (JRS) to coach players to win trophies upon trophies. He was able to spot talents and buy and sell players using transferrable skills (TS) possessed by anyone involved in huge financial transactions. He also demonstrated immense self-management skills (SMS) over a 26-year period when he had to deal with several players, club owners, Manchester United FC Board, the Football Association (FA), referees, irate club fans (when he wasn't winning) and supporters' clubs. On a few occasions, his emotions and frustrations got the better part of him and he received a five-match touchline ban in March 2011 after his team lost 2-1 to Chelsea FC. But for the most part, Ferguson was a man with admirable skills set who achieved great results during his tenure at Manchester United FC.

TRANSFERABLE SKILLS

You can transfer these skills from one type of work to another with little or no training regardless of the type of work. These include skills to act, adapt, advise, assess, audit, delegate, guide, lead, manage – people, resources, and time; direct, arrange, evaluate, coordinate, support, review, administrate, negotiate, communicate, train, and verify. Having these skills in relevant industries can determine whether people engage with your service or whether they overlook, bypass or ignore you.

Broadly, transferable skills can be sub-categorised under the following:

1. Managerial and administrative skills
2. Engagement and negotiating skills
3. Leadership skills

Managerial and Administrative Skills

These are sets of transferable skills used in running organisations, establishments and governmental institutions. Three examples to drive this home include:

Government - often seen in cabinet reshuffle across the world – for example, a Minister of Education redeployed to head the Energy and Petroleum resources ministry.

Corporate world - move by high ranking business executives from one industry to another – for example Angela Ahrendts moved from Burberry to Apple in 2014. She had exchanged the handbags business for one that makes handsets.

Administration and management - former English Football Association (FA) CEO Adam Crozier went to head the Post Office after leaving the English Football Association, and then later media group ITV in the UK. Dr Kofi Anan, the respected Ghanaian diplomat who served as the seventh Secretary-General of the United Nations from January 1997 to December 2006, previously worked in human resources, management, planning, budget and finance before becoming the top man at the United Nations.

Engagement and Negotiating Skills

Engagement and negotiating skills are types of transferable skills and are a must if you or your staffs want to represent your organization in the best possible way. This can make or break you or your staff or become the determining factor in what you do. You need people of understanding and skill to engage with your customers, clients or congregation in order to achieve positive outcomes. Great multinationals commanding millions and billions of dollars don't play with engagement and negotiation skills especially when large sums of money are involved.

I am reminded of the intense process that companies such as Cadbury and Kraft undergo to seal multimillion dollar deals. Rosneft and BP are other examples. Concerning the former, in the year 2009/10, Kraft Foods finally won the support of shareholders for the takeover of UK confectioner Cadbury, who agreed to a $19.5 billion deal. During the protracted (some would say hostile) takeover, Kraft constantly manoeuvred their offer to counter Cadbury's resistance and later bought the company – making Cadbury the largest chocolatier in the world.

What these multinationals do is to send out their best negotiators, who have skills and understanding. These skilled negotiators do their homework and understand business and operational etiquette, rules, protocols and the laws. They are clear about the terms of engagement, what exactly they are negotiating and why. They know how to approach their counterparts, know when to deploy hardline (not aggression or attack) or soft tactics, when to apply pressure, when to back down, when to call a bluff, and when to walk away from a deal. These people also understand *due dilligence.*

Leadership Skills

Leadership skills are transferable sets of skills that can be adapted and used in almost any setting. Readers who want to have a quick overview of essential leadership skills and attributes will find free resources under **Leadership Now** at www.profsexperts.com.

SELF MANAGEMENT SKILLS

These skills tell the employer about you, and whether you fit the job. These include being bold, adaptable, organised, punctual, clever, quick, flexible, frank, honest, helpful, determined, dedicated, dependable, friendly, clear-thinking, imaginative, energetic, logical, and methodical. The list is endless!

Skills that employers want
- Basic skills in reading, writing, and computation
- Basic financial and business literacy

- Communication skills (verbal [listening and speaking] and non-verbal [use of body language]
- Ability to learn and be teachable
- Problem solving, being creative and diversifying
- Goal setting, planning and achieving
- Personal, people and career development skills
- Interpersonal, negotiation and teamwork skills
- Organisational and leadership skills
- Appropriate social skills

And, I can go on. These skills can all be used for positive change. Your skills might include administrative, leadership, managerial, hospitality, event management, decorating, social networking, financial, negotiation, conflict resolution, mediation, media and communication skills. Unless you look critically, you may think you have little or nothing to offer. You don't have to be an expert. Do something today!

HOW TO ACQUIRE SKILLS

01. You can gain skills through specific training

This includes formal training and apprenticeships. You will need to undergo the necessary training to be competent in whatever you want to do. Needless to say, if you want to be a pilot, you will need to go to a pilot training school. During your training, you will be taught about how aircrafts work, various aspects of flying and landing a plane, how to fly at night and in turbulent weather conditions, and also responding to all sorts of emergencies. You will then be assessed, first with simulator machines that pretend to be actual aircrafts in an environment that presents something like the real flying environment. You will have to sit theory and practical examinations before you can be certified to be a safe pilot. The same goes for if you want to train to be a doctor or a nurse.

In some professions, training is achieved through apprenticeship, a combination of formal and on the job training. If you want to be a professional dancer, you will have to go to a dance school, or a master baker, you will have get into a kitchen to learn to bake bread or cake. You can read scores of books about journalism but until you actually go out to interview and talk to people, you will not become a journalist. Also reading about the history of music is good; and music production conferences, courses and seminars will go a long way, but in the end, to be a music producer, you will have to get into a studio to learn through apprenticeships first-hand, from people who are already in the industry.

In the UK, useful information can be accessed via websites such as www.apprenticeships.gov.uk and www.nationalcareersservice.direct.gov.uk. In essence, whatever field you find work, you first have to receive training in the theory of what underpins the working of a particular task. You then have to translate that theory into practice and then aim to be a competent practitioner. This must necessarily be followed by continuous training to keep your skill updated and fresh, and move with new development through life time learning.

02. You can gain skills through recreation

Recreation often provides an avenue for excitement, fun and adventure but also can be a useful platform for acquiring and developing personal and interpersonal skills, confidence, practical knowledge or expertise. Some recreational clubs are targeted towards direct skills acquisition such as sewing, knitting, and even web design. I have in the past asked people to join a Math or Computer Club for fun in other to improve their skill in Mathematics or Computers. Review your hobbies or whatever you do as a volunteer. Are there skills that you can develop and apply more widely?

03. Copy what has worked elsewhere

You don't really have to reinvent the wheel. This is the famous catch phrase from Evan Carmichaels: *"I believe the best way to grow your business is to model people that are already successful in what you are trying to do."* I referred to this earlier as 'Modeling the Masters'. To learn from people ahead in any endeavor, you will need to be specific in your quest, determined in your approach, and persistent in your pursuit. Without these mindsets, you will be easily discouraged. A person who is arrogant, full of pride and not humble cannot learn from others.

04. Work for somebody for free

One of the smartest things you can do is to work for others for free. It doesn't matter what the project is, working in projects can teach people about critical workplace skills such as technical expertise, delegation, communication and leadership skills. If you want to be an entrepreneur, you want to learn from a successful one. Go and work for free. Get as involved as much as you can be in the business and think about what you would do in similar situations as the owner.

Don't be discouraged if the first job you are asked to do is to make tea or carry the papers (or bags); do your work with all diligence. Doing what some people might consider mundane may actually get you close to the right people. Actually, this is how many successful actors started. Before you know it, you will start handling the camera, arranging meetings or sorting out the policy papers for the CEO. Put your heart in whatever you do. And before you know it, you are on the next plane to represent the Director of Policy and Research when the boss cannot make the meeting. Don't forget: you are working here for the experience and education, not for the money. The money will come when you get appointed into your own job or set up your own business.

05. Volunteering formally

This can be arranged to suit already known work or family life patterns while you are acquiring skills that current or future employers will value much later. The following are the benefits of volunteering:

- Enables you to use your spare time more constructively.

- Helps you develop the confidence to try out different roles and careers.

- Volunteering positions could offer bespoke training.

- Enhances job prospects. Employers more likely to hire

people with volunteering experience than those without.

- Helps to plug gaps in your CV while offering opportunity for developing skills.
- Volunteering undoubtedly helps with work experience, contacts and references.
- Helps unemployed people get back to work.
- Volunteering make positive difference in the lives of people who benefit from the services provided for free.
- Helps identify other career opportunities or pathway that you may not have considered before.

06. Networking

Irrespective of the field of industry or area of business, networking can be the key to success. By networking, you acquire skills of how things are done in certain settings. You can learn how to strike up impromptu conversations with strangers by networking. You may be able to gain more clients, exchange information and learn from peers.

07. Practical skills from seemingly adverse experience and situation

I once attended a two-day Root Cause Analysis* (RCA) training of which one of the facilitators was a nurse whose former place of work had faced a lengthy enquiry after a series of adverse incidents. While her department was being scrutinized years before, the nurse had observed that the investigators were very methodical and rigorous in their

---

*Root Cause Analysis is a method of problem solving which addresses the root causes of faults or problems.

approach. After the enquiry, she left her employment to set up a consultancy firm advising organisations on how best to support and to advise staff facing similar enquiries. Her company grew into one that conducts RCAs around the country looking into adverse situations and incidents and recommending how to spot early warning signs that things could go wrong, how to manage near misses and how to prevent future adverse and risky incidents.

From a prisoner to a prime minister

Joseph, the son of Jacob in the Bible was another person who exemplified how skills could be acquired even during bad times. Joseph was sold into slavery by his brothers; he was bought at the slave market by Portiphar, a very senior official of Pharaoh, the King of Egypt. Joseph was put in charge of other staff in Portiphar's court. That role meant he had to look after Portiphar's entire household, manage staff and look after their welfare and everything belonging to Portiphar. He would have been privy to the goings in the courtyard of a high ranking official of the king, and giving account was part of his role. That was until he was wrongly sent to jail for 'refusing to sleep' with his boss' wife.

Again while in jail, Joseph became the head (or chief) prisoner responsible for managing other prisoners, and reported to the chief jailer. Joseph was again exposed to administration and management at the time. As it happened, the king had a problem; Pharaoh's dream had to be interpreted, which Joseph did with the help of God.

So when Pharaoh appointed Joseph as the Prime Minister in Egypt at the age of 30, administration and management were not new to him. He acquired those transferable skills when he was a slave without any hope of being released.

7 WAYS TO MAXIMISE YOUR SKILLS

Discover – Identify your skills. Find out what you can do and to what extent. Think of all the things you can do reasonably well and list the skills that enable you to do them. Include the things you do with ease and those that others commend you for.

Develop – Develop and refine your skills through further education, training and practice. It is always good to benchmark with what is the current best practice or standard in the industry.

Decision – Decide to do something with your skills. Don't wait until somebody or an organisation says you are an expert. Not that there is anything wrong in being validated by others as an expert, but if you have something to give, offer it.

Determine – Target your skills towards something very productive, and never give in when opposition arises.

Deploy – Put your skills to work by marketing them, both for monetary and non-monetary reasons. Look for the right people and environment and ask: "Who needs what I've got?" "Who requires my skills and for what?" Take (or offer) your skills to where they are needed. Meet a need.

Distribute – Spread your skills, near and far by identifying and seizing opportunities. Also use the power of technology and the internet to put yourself out there.

Donate – Give your skills for free. You are blessed to be a blessing. A little and seemingly insignificant contribution from what you have can make a whole lot of difference to those who benefit from it.

HOW TO BECOME HIGHLY SKILLED
RESPECT what you have.

R – Research – The word *Re-Search* has two parts. *Re* – means to do it and do it again; and to *Search* implies to look closely, to dig deeper, to find out and to go beyond the surface. Research enriches what you already have.

E – Educate – Train your mind by exposing it to information, ideas and processes. This can be formal or informal.

S – Study – Apply your mind to understanding a topic, a particular object, item, product, concept or subject matter to find out what constitutes the basis of its existence, composition or operation. It is in the process of studying that you attain a better understanding, innovate (or stumble upon) and develop new ideas.

P – Practice – Work and act on what you already know. Improve on it, and before you know it you will become a specialist or an expert. The Oxford Dictionary defines an expert as "a person who is very knowledgeable about or skilful in a particular area." Expertise can only be achieved when you practice and continue to improve what you do.

E – Evaluate– Examine and continue to review what you do and figure out how to make it better. Determine areas that need improving and do something about them. According to Socrates, "The unexamined life is not worth living."

C – Cultivate – Provide yourself with an environment where you can flourish. Traditional cultivation requires a seed, the soil, work and time. Your idea and skill set are the seed, the soil is the environment in which you place (or plant) yourself. You have to go through a process over time to achieve mastery. And, don't forget the rain, the blessing of God.

T – Teach– Show others what you know. You are likely to retain 70-90 percent of what you teach. Even though I sat for and passed GCSE 'O' Level subjects in June 1985, I have continued to teach Mathematics, Physics, Chemistry, Biology, Physical Education and Food technology up till now and my knowledge of these subjects remain intact even at the present time.

HINTS FOR SKILLS

Percentage Retention Based on Action Performed	
Action performed	Percentage retention
What you read	10%
What you hear	20%
What you see	30%
What you see and hear	50%
What you say or teach	70%
What you say and do	90%

Asking the right questions

- What skills do I have? *Look inwards.*
- What do others think I am good at? *Listen carefully.*
- Where have I used this skill before? *Check carefully.*
- What can I do that others cannot do? *Nothing, really.*
- How can I use my skills differently? *Leverage them appropriately.*

- How can I refine my skills? *Training and development.*
- Who can benefit from and buy my skills? *Customers and society.*
- How much is my skill worth? *Pricing and costing.*
- How can I sell my skills? *Create an invoice and get paid.*
- How can I ensure the business continues? *Think sustainability and succsess.*

3 Things I Will Do Today

1. Think carefully of at least one skill I have that can be better put to use.

2. Make a concrete plan to develop one of my skills to solve particular problems.

3. Explore definite ways to acquire one or two more skills in addition to what I already have.

T
TIME

Time

Definition: Time is the system of those sequential relations that any event has to any other, as past, present, or future; indefinite and continuous duration regarded as that in which events succeed one another.

O f all the five attributes this book deals with, time is the only one that is totally external to an individual. God has given every one of us time in equal measure and also the freewill to choose how we spend it. Therefore, no one should complain saying "I haven't got time" or ask "Where's the time gone?" Come to think of it: time is the only irreplaceable asset that every man has. Once it's gone, it's gone! Therefore today, you must consciously think on how you spend your time. Think about it.

Time is the only true currency of life. If you are employed in a job, you start work at a certain time and you finish at a particular time. Provided you actually deliver, you are paid a certain amount of money at the end of the day, week or month – for spending six, eight or 10 hours of your life each day in your job. In essence, your employer pays you for spending your time, for instance, eight hours daily of your adult life working for them. Essentially what you have exchanged for the money paid to you (or that you pay yourself if you are self-employed) is your time - I mean a portion of your life.

"Time is a currency of life; many people spend it without knowing."

Have you noticed yet? There are too many things – to do; there is too much information – to handle; there is too much responsibility – to bear; and yet there is not enough time. You must realise that time waits for no man. Some would say, "Time is gone,"but this is not true. Time is just there; it hasn't gone anywhere. It is down to us whether we use it well or not.

P-A-R-T-S of a 24-Hour Clock

The 24-hour clock is one of the instruments that I use when I am trying to drive home a point about the importance of using time wisely. The PARTS of your 24-hour day must be devoted to Planning, Activities, Rest, Tasks (goal-oriented), and Sleep. These components form the acronym P-A-R-T-S*.

PLANNING

No matter how busy you are, a reasonable part of your day should be devoted to planning how you will spend it.

*The P-A-R-T-S Clockface. Copyright by Muyiwa Olumoroti 2015

A well planned day and routine has a lesser chance of being intruded upon. If you don't plan, your day is already at the mercy of chaos and unscheduled activities, some of which are legitimate. Also there are people going nowhere who want to spend their day with you. So, plan your day.

ACTIVITIES

There are only four main activities that you do with your time, really. You sit, stand 'soar' or sleep. What different people do in these positions vary. However, you must never mistake activity for productivity.

Sit

One of the best things you can do with your time when you sit is to meditate and be quiet in order to afford yourself some time to think. Quietness is one of the arts of personal and spiritual discipline that have been lost in our busy and rowdy world–a world where everything and everyone is calling for your attention. Quietness and thinking allow you to plan and to focus. Focus is one of the greatest attributes of great inventors. It was said of Isaac Newton, that most of his successes had to do with his ability to focus intensely on a particular problem until he found a solution.

Solitude and separation are two practices which must be cultivated if you want to perform at the cutting edge of your vocation. You can also read, meditate, strategise and process knowledge when you find a quiet place to reflect and an environment to ask the right questions. It is rare and almost impossible to think or meditate when you are sleeping, and certainly almost impossible to achieve anything meaningful whilst you are restless and jumping about on your feet. Most productive work is done when people sit down to actually do the work they are being paid for.

Stand

Whether you take this literally or not, the time that you stand is when you rise up to a purpose or a challenge. And, if you don't stand up for something, you will fall for anything. An idle hand, some people say, is the devil's workshop. So, do something with your hand, and your brain. Make a difference and be productive. Stand up and be counted.

Soar

Most people don't literarily soar for long, unless you are a bird or perpetually suspended in space. The time to soar is the time invested to move on to the next level, be it reading, studying, researching, planning or experimenting. Your value for time determines the value you have for your life. Only people who make the most of their time make the most of their life. What are you really doing with your time today?

Soaring with time: *The story of Gates, Zuckerberg and D'Aloisio*

William Henry "Bill" Gates III

Bill Gates ranked as the richest man in the world in 2015 with an estimated fortune of $79.2 billion. Mr Gates came from an upper-middle-class family, and went to one of the few schools with computers in the 1970s. Computers have always been his thing, and he was often excused from Math classes to pursue his interests in computers. He later dropped out of Harvard at the age of 19 to start Microsoft, with his friend, Paul Allen. In 2007, Gates was later awarded an honorary doctorate from Harvard, from where he had dropped out as an undergraduate three decades earlier.

In July 2014, when Bill Gates received an honorary degree from Addis Ababa University in Ethiopia, he responded after his introduction: "I am deeply grateful for this honorary degree. I never got my real degree. I dropped out to start Microsoft, and never went back. So getting a diploma I can put on the wall and show my father is a relief." Unlike many drop-outs, Bill Gates did not spend his time hanging around the streets of New Mexico with riff-raffs; he linked up with like-minded individuals to pursue his dream. A very wise use of his time paid off huge 'dividends' for him as a result.

Mark Zuckerberg

Most likely you would know or have read about Facebook. Mark Zuckerberg created a media player called *Synapse* when he was about the age of 18 while still in school. He later went to Harvard University where he set up Facebook from his college room. His net worth was estimated to be in the region of $33 billion after there was a surge in Facebook stock in August 2014.

Nick D'Aloisio

Most parents would probably be worried if their teenagers lock themselves up in their bedroom working or playing on their computers. However, some teenagers have been known to turn into good use, time spent on computer and mobile devices in recent times. Nick D'Aloisio was looking for ways to absorb large amounts of information while studying for history exams at the age of 15 when he was inspired to create *Summly*. D'Aloisio, from an idea he worked on from his bedroom, created an application for iOS (a mobile operating system) in March 2011, which condenses very large text content into 1,000, 500, or 140-character summary text. Aged 17, D'Aloisio, sold *Summly*, an app that summarises news stories from media websites, to Yahoo in 2013 in a deal said to be in the range of $30 million. To me that was a very good use and investment of time.

REST

Rest forms part of the acronym P-A-R-T-S, and it is important that plan for your time includes time for rest.

Everybody needs rest, particularly after a period of work or exertion. Rest allows your mind to re-charge and refresh in preparation for more reasonable use of your time. Some people  consider sleep alone as rest but the two are not necessarily the same. Rest can come in form of leisure, relaxing, meditating, and spending time with others.

TASKS (Goal-oriented)

Your time is your life, and how you spend it is up to you. People sometimes become busy during recessions and austere times, trying to make ends meet, either by taking up more jobs, working longer hours, thereby having little or no time for others including their families. Working harder or longer in itself is not a problem as long as you have the correct perspective and you are able to strike the right balance. Be careful not to spend more and more of your time pursuing things that bring only little rewards. Come to think of it, that is your life you are spending, not someone else's. It is not just about what you do or how much effort you put in, or even your will but it is God who causes a man or woman to prosper. In other words, hard work is good, but in itself does not make you rich.

SLEEP

An average person sleeps about 7-10 hours a day. Some sleep less, and some sleep more. You can't do much in your sleep except have pleasant and sweet dreams, or nightmares that you hope to wake up from! So, logically, if you can't achieve much in your sleep, except for the benefit of feeling refreshed from the required sleep time, then it is safe to conclude that you will be wasting a precious part of your life if you sleep all day.

I have put below some illustrations on how much sleep one needs lest somebody says, "You don't understand; I need my sleep." The body has been engineered in such a way that

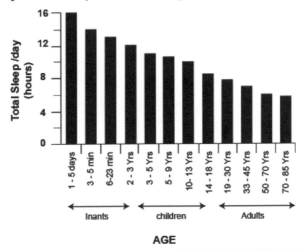

it demands the sleep it requires. So, sleeping too much is a waste of time.

AGE OR CONDITION	SLEEP NEEDED
Newborn (0–2 months)	12 to 18 hours
Infants (3–11 months)	14 to 15 hours
Toddlers (1–3 years)	12 to 14 hours
Preschoolers (3–5 years)	11 to 13 hours
School-age children (5–10 years)	10 to 11 hours
Adolescents (10–17 years)	8.5 to 9.25 hours
Adults, including elderly	7 to 9 hours
Pregnant women	8(+) hours

From http://www.odec.ca/projects/2005/rich5a0/public_html/sleep2.bmp

DON'T SLEEP YOUR LIFE AWAY

A star student is not made in the class but after the class has ended. They burn the midnight oil and they become friends with stars that rise at night; and when other people are sleeping, they put in the extra hours that make them excel. People who know how to invest in the night are the ones who will rule during the day. The accounts of the sleep lives of men and women who have excelled in their various field of endeavour will make you think again.

Margaret Thatcher, former British Prime Minister, was popularly quoted as saying she slept for only four hours a night. President Bill Clinton was widely quoted as saying he slept between five to six hours a night during his presidency and President Obama was recently reported to be averaging about six hours a night. Dr David Oyedepo, the Presiding Bishop of the Living Faith Church Worldwide (also known as Winners' Chapel International) is reported to work an average of about 18 hours a day and sleeps for around four to six hours a night. Without fail, these people get things done.

Less sleep does not ensure success but too much sleep would almost guarantee failure.

Myles Munroe said if we sleep an average eight hours a day, it means we sleep 56 hours a week. That is, we sleep at least for two days (plus another eight hours) each week. Can you imagine how much you can get done if you sleep less? If you sleep an average of eight hours per day over a hundred year period, you would have slept for a whopping 33 years of your life. The first time Anjola, my 9 year-old-daughter, read this statement about sleep, she said: "What!!! Why Daddy? 33 years is too much time to sleep!" I said: "Exactly!" Think about it.

DO YOU SLEEP A LOT?

If You Live for

100 years

and **sleep** for an average

8 Hours a day (apart from the time you slept (more) as a baby or an infant), you would have slept for

33

Years of Your Life

DO YOU WANT TO BE A CEO?

I studied the wake-up times of seven Chief Executive Officers of major organisations - AOL, Virgin Money, MediaCom UK, Ericsson, Newton Investment, Vodafone and the non-executive director of the UK Football Association (FA) - interviewed by *The Guardian Newspapers* (UK edition; Monday April 1, 2013). Their wake-up times range from 5am to 6.20am. I calculated the average wake-up time to be 5.43am for the CEOs. These high fliers wake up very early and certainly don't sleep all day. In the words of Mr Donald

Trump, the chairman of The Trump Organization (as quoted in the *Daily News*, Friday, June 26, 2009): "How does somebody that's sleeping 12 and 14 hours a day compete with someone that's sleeping three or four?" It's a no brainer.

ASPECTS OF TIME

There are different aspects of time, and I am referring to: **Chronos, Kairos, Keeping time and Aeons**.

CHRONOS

This refers to a space of time or the passage of time and this is the commonest use of the word, time. It is time in terms of a sequence, for example, one second or minute following another. Remember the words 'chronometer', 'chronology' or 'chronic'. 'Chronos', you hear things such as slow, fast or quick and sluggish. You must take advantage of time as you cannot buy it back.

Did you know?

- 1 minute (or several days) is lost looking for a passport.
- 1 to 2 minutes is spent looking for your car keys.
- 4 minutes is lost looking for a misplaced or lost lottery ticket.
- 5 minutes a day is wasted looking for remote

controllers.

- 7 minutes are spent looking for socks and shoes.

- 10 minutes are spent looking for lost or misplaced keys.

- 10-16 minutes a day are wasted looking for lost possessions – that is over 177 days over a lifetime.

- 17 minutes are spent shouting, "You had it last!"

- 55 minutes per day is spent by Americans looking for things they know they own but cannot find.

Time Waits For No Man!

Life is measured in time; how we live it, and how we end it. Time is the most important factor in this world. Time is precious and invaluable. When you don't have it, you can't do much! Time never stops and does not wait for anyone. If you lose time, you can't regain it back. You may be able to redeem time but you can never repeat it. You can't hold time neither can it be captured. You can't slow time down and you can't hasten it either. The rich and the powerful have all been at the mercy of time and cannot stop it or buy it. Once it is gone, it is gone forever.

Time is not even yours; it is given to all. Everything and everyone is commanded and decided by time. So, you have to be careful how you spend time. Don't waste time. That is life you are toying with. When you have the opportunity, use time to your advantage. Use those opportunities to move on and move forward. A wise person maximises the times of their life; a foolish person squanders time away. Invest your time in your future because that is where you will spend the rest of your life. Decide today that you will make time work for you. Don't be left out.

Accomplish

Time is needed for accomplishments in life. It takes time for things to happen. Some things just have to run their course and take their time in order to reach their full potential or for one to actualise. Just as seeds need time to grow, so also babies in the womb require about nine months to grow to maturity. Anything short of that, there could be a miscarriage or premature birth. Anything more than nine months, there is post-maturity and risks of complications. You also need time to prepare yourself to take hold of the promises of life. Without preparation, opportunities will go to waste. Accomplishment is impossible without commitment, your education notwithstanding.

> *"Every accomplishment in life is a product of investment of time."*
> -Dr David Oyedepo, President, Living Faith Church worldwide.

How to maximise your time

- Plan for today. Have a daily to-do or task list.
- Plan for tomorrow; plan for the day after next.
- Do the hardest and most important things first.
- Set expectations, manage priorities.

- Set deadlines. Check what has been achieved.

- Adopt new ways of working - work smarter, not harder.

- Avoid time wasters – see examples below.

- Manage time spent on emails, text messages, Internet and social media. Go offline for some time in order to focus on priorities. It won't kill you!

- Know how to say "No." Everything is not important.

- Take a break. You will be surprised what you can achieve after a rest period.

- Use time to get relevant information. Invest your time in what will pay dividends later.

Time wasters - you know them!

1. Complaining about everything without doing anything.

2. Gossiping and getting in other people's way.

3. Doing other people's work or busy body or day dreaming.

4. Excessive TV, video games, online chats and overuse of social media.

5. Not being decisive and procrastinating.

6. Reading tabloid news, and following celebrities or the so-called world news.

7. Antagonizing, plotting, scheming or setting traps for

others.

8. Waiting for something bad to happen to others or trying to prove a point.

9. Unnecessary meetings after meetings; unplanned, cancellations and postponements.

10. Answering all phone calls or attending to every e-mail notification and text messages.

11. Lack of organization and looking for misplaced items.

12. Random tasking or working, and not having or working to a 'To-do-list'.

"We all have a limited time, but what we can do within that time is unlimited."

What to do when you are stuck in a place

You must remain productive when you find yourself in a situation you cannot get out of quickly. I went to work at a Category B prison in London in 2005. The first thing my consultant said to me was: "You must have a way of doing something when there is nothing to do in this place." When you work in a prison environment, situations could arise when the prison becomes 'locked down', either due to a security emergency or when a prisoner could not be accounted for. All activities are suspended except breathing. Nothing moves in or out of that prison until that prisoner is found or accounted for somehow, even it means the prisoner has escaped (very rare) or fallen asleep in a workshop toilet. A security situation could be resolved in a matter of minutes but could also last hours; and if the latter ever happened, I made sure I had a pen and a notebook on me to do some work while the standstill lasted.

The value of time

You never know the value of time until you are stuck in a place and cannot do anything with all the time you have. But some people have been good at making use of their time such as the examples below.

Apostle Paul (otherwise called St. Paul) wrote some of his epistles when he was in one prison or the other. **Joseph (son of Jacob)** in the Bible was also productive while in prison, and he ended up becoming the Prime Minister in Egypt.

Chief Obafemi Awolowo (1909- 1987) (Senior Advocate of Nigeria). Wrote *'My March Through Prison'* while he was incarcerated.

Nelson Mandela wrote *Conversations with Myself*, a scrapbook-style piece of work chronicling Mandela's life during his 27 years in prison.

Martin Luther King Jr. wrote Letters from Birmingham Jail following his imprisonment for organizing a non-violent protest against racial segregation in Alabama.

Vicky Pryce, formerly chief economist at Royal Bank of Scotland, UK, wrote *Prisonomics* out of her two-month experience in prison following her conviction for perverting the course of justice.

Good things can actually come out of adverse situations, when time is well spent. Time wasted is actually life wasted. So keep working, like the Big Ben.

The Big Ben

Big Ben is the nickname for the Great Bell of the clock at the north end of the Palace of Westminster (or the Houses of Parliament) in London. The Big Ben, come rain or sunshine, has been working for over 150 years except for brief periods of interruption. So keep on w o r k i n g; don't waste your time - I mean your life.

GOOD TIME -KEEPING

A man who cannot keep time cannot be serious with anything. If you ask some people to see you for an important appointment at 9.30am, you will be deemed lucky if they show up by 12 noon. To make it worse, these people don't even realise they have done anything wrong. They walk in late as a matter of fact, and give you a very pitiful 'sorry' for wasting your time. People who cannot keep time and are always late are often seen as slackers; other people have a negative impression of them. They quickly lose admirers and become a clog in the wheel of progress of others. These people think they are the only ones that have challenges in life, and give excuse after excuse. You must never be a man or woman like that.

KAIROS

The other aspect of time is referred to as 'Kairos' or the right or auspicious moment of time. This refers to a moment in time, a fixed time, a decisive moment, the right time, an opportune time, the appointed time, or the fullness of time. God has an appointed time for everything, and there is a time for every purpose under the sun.

"To everything there is a season, A time for every purpose under heaven. "
Ecclesiastes 3:1- The Bible

You have to be prepared for 'Kairos' otherwise you might miss your window of opportunity. Kairos is about 'seizing the moment', and a lot has been written on this in this book in the chapter titled Opportunities. Life has no rewind button; an opportunity missed may never be regained. Many times, we miss out on today's possibilities because we are reflecting on the 'good old days' and living on past glories. When you need to act today, you can't decide not to move until tomorrow. You cannot afford to procrastinate or prevaricate or postpone. If you don't act now, the people next to you might. Planning is what gives value to your time and resources and ultimately, your life pursuits. So, be prepared.

Kairos also refers to a season, an appropriate time, or a timely period or interval. If you are the type that watches animal documentaries, for example on the National Geographic TV channel, you will probably have seen when migratory animals - large or small, especially birds, who at one time were flourishing in a habitat or an environment conducive to their survival, procreation, protection, and provision for food, decide to move on. As soon as the climate changes and the water level in rivers or lakes begins to fall, these animals begin to migrate. Some birds travel in groups, sometimes up to thousands of kilometres, in order to adapt to the changes around them.

Migratory birds and other animals are very sensitive. Something in their brains or in their body (which is wired to their brain), tells them, "Birds, it's time to move!" Call it remote control or a sensor, the God Almighty is the one that put it there. Something in the animals' brains tells the birds: 'We can't stay on this tree (or mountain, or brook, or drying lake) any longer. There is a promise of a better life for us on the other side and we need to cross over, now!' And these animals are not only sensitive, they are smart, and they cross over in good time, before it is too late.

Punctual To Seasons

"Even the migratory birds are punctual to their seasons. Yes, the stork [excelling in the great height of her flight] in the heavens knows her appointed times [of migration], and the turtledove, the swallow, and the crane observe the time of their return. But My people do not know the law of the Lord [which the lower animals instinctively recognize in so far as it applies to them]."
Jeremiah 8: 7 The Amplified Bible

Without fail, those animals that refuse to move are the ones that eventually perish in the wilderness. This is the same with humans: there are times, when if you introduce things too quickly, you spoil the impact. Also when you act too slowly, you are exposed and leave yourself vulnerable, or miss out altogether. When the time for your promise comes, you shouldn't remain where you are; you should migrate to where you should be, in your thinking, in your planning and in your actions.

Kairos is about opportunities, seizing the moment and making the necessary moves. The twelve reasons why people miss or misuse opportunities have been discussed under the chapter titled 'Opportunities' on page 65.

A LIFE'S CONVERSATION

Life has no rewind button;
it is best to make use of the
time you have today.

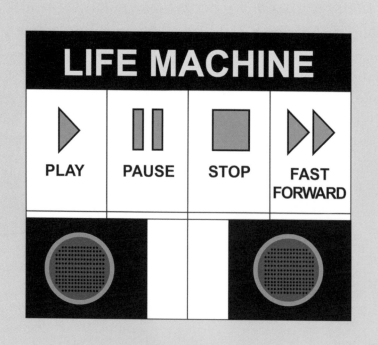

Sir, I have come to return this machine;
it has no REWIND button.
I am so sorry, that's how it's made.

AEONS

Aeons refers to an interval of time or an age. This usually speaks of dispensations of time, for example scores, hundreds or even thousands of years. Time moves on and nothing stands still. The only thing that is permanent is change itself. So if you don't move with time, you will be left behind.

Following on from the Stone Age or the Ice Age, the world civilisation has been defined as the Agrarian Age which persisted until about 1860. During that time, land was the main source of wealth and agriculture was the occupation of 90 per cent of the population. The Industrial Age followed from about 1860 to 1956 and this was characterised by the invention of the steam engine, technological advancement, and manufacturing in factories with machines. The world then moved from that period to what has been popularly described as the Information Age, from about 1956 to date.

An extension of the Information Age is the Digital Age and the Shift Age – where information changes, and is updated by the minutes and seconds on the Internet, CNN, Sky, Fox News, or Aljazeera News Network. We no longer write on paper, but on personal computers, laptops, smart phones and tablets. Now you can fit 1,000 eBooks in a memory stick or CD-ROM or on an iPad! The next time you wait for a parcel to be delivered, expect an aerial drone rather than a postman. Even wars have moved away from spears and daggers to the realm of cyber wars!

3 Things I Will Do Today

1. Make a list of activities you are spending time on but not producing much. Get rid of those endeavours.

2. Make a list of things you have wanted to do according to priority, and then, get on with them.

3. Write down four things you will now consider as time-wasters. Eliminate them.

Closing thoughts

Do Something Today

TOAST stands for Talents (and gifts), Opportunities, Abilities (and strengths), Skills and Time. Just like many things you have heard or read before, we all know these things. It is only when we practice them that we achieve great results. The materials in TOAST are there to encourage you to consider, reflect and purposefully think about what you have been endowed with in order to maximise them. Don't think about what you don't have; look inwards, stretch yourself and bring out the best in you and from around you.

So, I am going to ask you to consciously think about TOAST. I do not intend to think it for you. I want you to consider the five components of TOAST and ask yourself these crucial questions: What should I be thinking about the gifts that I have or the talents that I have been endowed with? What should I do with the opportunities that I am presented with or come across day after day? What abilities do I possess or am I endowed with which can be used to deal with tasks, circumstances and challenges? How do I make the best use of the time (24 hours a day!) that I have been equally given like any other person? What are the skills that I currently possess that could help in my overall development and how can I deploy them to achieve the best for myself and others?

Only you can answer these questions, and if you need help or require assistance, you may wish to contact me through email (info@profsexperts.com) or attend a TOAST Empowerment Network (TEN) training near you. I wish you all the best.

TOAST Empowerment Network

In order to maximise the benefit and get the most out this book, it is strongly advised that you attend a TOAST Empowerment Network training near you.

For more information about on and off-site training, please contact the author via email at:

info@profsexperts.com or onetouchfmsolutionsltd@gmail.com OR visit www.profsexperts.com

I look forward to hearing from you.

Dr Muyiwa Olumoroti MBBS, MSc, MRCPsych

.

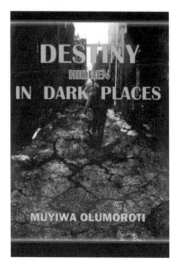

Destiny Hidden in Dark
Places
ISBN: 9781908588005

Patient Management
Problems in Psychiatry
ISBN: 9780443101618

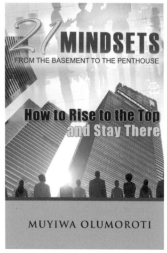

21 Mindsets - How to Rise to
the Top and Stay There
ISBN: 9781908588180

21 Mindsets - How to Stay
on Top and Achieve Maxi-
mum Impact at Work
ISBN: 9781908588135